# THE HEROIC HEART

# THE HEROIC HEART
## GREATNESS ANCIENT AND MODERN

### TOD LINDBERG

Encounter Books · New York · London

First American edition published in 2015 by Encounter Books,
an activity of Encounter for Culture and Education, Inc.,
a nonprofit, tax exempt corporation.
Encounter Books website address: www.encounterbooks.com

Manufactured in the United States and printed on
acid-free paper. The paper used in this publication meets
the minimum requirements of ANSI/NISO Z39.48–1992
(R 1997) (*Permanence of Paper*).

FIRST AMERICAN EDITION

LIBRARY OF CONGRESS CATALOGING-IN-PUBLICATION DATA
Lindberg, Tod.
The heroic heart: greatness ancient and modern/by Tod Lindberg.
pages cm
Includes bibliographical references and index.
ISBN 978-1-59403-823-5 (hardcover: alk. paper)—ISBN 978-1-59403-824-2 (ebook)
1. Conduct of life. 2. Heroes. I. Title.
BJ1533.H47L56 2015
205—dc23
2015005296

*For David Robins*

# CONTENTS

# INTRODUCTION

*. . . tho'*
*We are not now that strength which in old days*
*Moved earth and heaven, that which we are, we are;*
*One equal temper of heroic hearts,*
*Made weak by time and fate, but strong in will*
*To strive, to seek, to find, and not to yield.*
*—Tennyson, "Ulysses"*

I present to you a book I have been working on all my life, though not until recently with a view that the problems I was trying to figure out would turn into a book one day.

Do you have someone you consider to be your hero? Did you ever? Do you consider anyone, living or dead, to exemplify in one way or another the quality of greatness? I do, and did, and do.

And if you happen to be inclined to devote ten minutes to making a list of the people you have considered exceptionally admirable at one time or another in your life, I think your list no less than mine would form a proper beginning for an investigation of the qualities that make a hero—exemplary figures of human greatness, contemporary or historical, real or quasi-mythical or imaginary.

What a variety of characters populate my list of heroes. Who looms large? My parents, first of all: In the absence of tragic circumstances, early childhood seems inevitably to ascribe larger-than-life stature to Mom and Dad. Then comes an inevitable period of ups and downs, middle school emphatically included. Later, if all goes well, comes a grown-up appreciation of who they were and what they did for you. In my case, that turned out to have been a lot more than they were under any reasonable obligation to do.

My mother was badly afflicted at an early age with rheumatoid arthritis, and the joints of her fingers were frozen into awkwardly painful positions. She and my father long wanted children, but the years went by without success, to the point at which hope was fleeting. I was a late-arriving surprise.

Stomach cancer, first misdiagnosed as an ulcer, claimed my mother in her late forties when I was about 13; it's unlikely given the state of treatment at the time that a proper diagnosis would have changed the outcome. Her battle did not last long.

I mention her lifelong adversity because my mother was undaunted by it until the end. She was a teacher, though not full-time once I came along; but as I got older she took longer-term assignments as a substitute. She was in high demand at an area school for special needs children, who were then called mentally retarded. I am not above a certain coarseness of expression. But from my earliest youth onward, the use of "retard" to refer to someone with disabilities has struck me much the way the N-word strikes decent people nowadays. It evokes visceral disgust. This is a legacy of my mother (who actually was a woman above coarseness of expression).

She was a natural leader and was good at most everything she did. I was bursting with pride when she became president of the Women's Club of White Oak Heights only a couple years after we moved to that suburban Pittsburgh neighborhood. Once her term was over, I liked to look at her name in the club's annual guidebook in the list of "Past Presidents." Her cooking was delicious beyond all expectation in the late 1960s; I retain to this day a taste memory of the shrimp Newburg she often made for company. As for her excellence in local bridge tournaments, usually playing with my father, I once asked Mom how well Dad knew the game; she sweetly replied that it didn't matter that much, because she knew Dad.

My father was an Eagle Scout, a rank I never attained, and he took over as scoutmaster of my troop as I was beginning to outgrow it, continuing for several years in the absence of any current scout father stepping up. He was a man without great ambition but reasonably successful in his career, working as a traffic agent moving coal for the railroad, eventually becoming Coal Sales Manager in Chicago, the final stop of four cities of increasing size in my youth.

That's where calamity struck with the death of my mother. I can't imagine what that must have been like for him. Not just the grief but the sudden onset of full responsibility—for me, that is: a newly minted teenager with no small sense of self and a sore grievance with Fate. We didn't talk about my mother until years later, and even then only rarely, usually under the influence of scotch-and-soda at some dive where Dad was screwing the lady bartender. He told me once that my mother's support was behind any success he'd had. "She lifted me up," he said, his face contorting and eyes welling with uncontainable tears.

The evident dissipation of his retirement years was, for me, an issue. Dad was then no hero. The furniture was falling to cigarette-burn ruin and the yard returning to prairie. I was embarrassed. But I was missing the point, which was that my father never gave a damn about material surroundings, just the people who inhabited them. When my mother was alive, the yard was immaculate. Now, there was a higher priority. Some people drink to forget, he once said; he drank to remember.

I was the principal beneficiary of his selflessness. It entailed such things as devoting the tax refund he got from losing his shirt on the stock he owned in his bankrupted railroad company, the Penn Central, to buy my garage band an expensive sound system. But I was hardly the only beneficiary. All of my Boy Scout buddies knew him as someone good for a drink and a pleasant evening of reminiscing and swapping tales—like the time on a camping trip when my friend T. spent the night passed out face down on a muddy path, followed by an amazing bout of puking the next morning. (Don't cut frozen lemonade concentrate with straight vodka, kids.) Dad never had much money, and what he did have he spent—not on himself but on others. His credo, though never articulated as such, was to take any given occasion and make more of it.

So, my heroes Mom and Dad. Also, Mr. H., the father of one of my friends and the coach of our Little League team, to me the very model of rectitude and probity. Not that I ever thought of him in those terms. But during one baseball season, another friend of mine, more advanced in the ways of the world, excitedly decided to tell me about the facts of life. He presented his information as if he'd been born with the knowledge: how the man's dick went into the woman's—well, I don't remember the term he used; "dick" is verbatim, though. As he went on, not that he had much else to say, I was pretending to have known about such matters all along. But internally I completely rejected my friend's outlandish claim. My reason for doing so was that Mr. H. came immediately to mind as a test case. It was simply inconceivable to me that Mr. H. had ever put his dick in my friend's mother. No. Never. Mr. H. would never do such a thing.

Mr. L. was my clarinet teacher in Pittsburgh, before we moved to Chicago. By the measure of my experience, he was exotic—a Jewish man who drove a huge black Cadillac and was the region's acknowledged master instructor in my instrument. I was a technically accomplished clarinetist for my young age, but Mr. L. didn't give a damn. Technique was the easy part. He cared about tone, and he meant to rebuild mine from scratch.

He matter-of-factly informed me early on that he didn't think I had the mouth structure to become a professional clarinetist; but he did think that with work, I could expect to become a good player. Although I had no plans at age 10 to become a professional musician, I was still crushed by his advance judgment of my inevitable failure. I resolved to put myself to the task. So we went about it for a couple of years, together once a week for half-an-hour-plus, working on my embouchure and the tone it produced.

My clarinet lessons were, unrelievedly, a difficult experience, as Mr. L.'s teaching style relied on correction of deficiency rather than praise of improvement. In truth, I wasn't sure how far I was getting—not until my very last lesson before my family moved to Chicago. Mr. L.'s small storefront studio consisted of an armchair for him and a straight-backed chair and music stand for his pupil at the far end, facing a ring of card table chairs around the three other walls for students (and parents of students) whose lessons were upcoming. Because he typically kept students past their scheduled half hour, Mr. L. was always running late. At the end of my last lesson, he turned to the younger girl who was next up for the pupil's chair and said to her something the like of which I had never heard from him before: "Doesn't he have a nice tone?" Ecstasy.

Those were some of my personal heroes. Do they remind you of any of yours? Of course I had heroes I shared with others. Books, whether true or fiction, provided most of them, including such worthies as George Washington, Abraham Lincoln, and Harriet Tubman, along with more remote characters such as David of biblical fame. In terms of preponderance of influence, this list would be seriously misleading without mention of Spider-Man.

Later on, I developed a high regard not only for some of the characters in books but also for the authors of certain books, including many quoted in the pages that follow. And actors in certain roles seemed at times to personify the greatness of the characters they played. How was it that George C. Scott playing Patton seemed somehow *more* Patton *than* Patton? Was Patton the hero—or Scott's Patton? Meanwhile, and back to reality, what can you say about a man like Chesley "Sully" Sullenberger, who landed his crippled and crashing Airbus A320 *in the middle of the Hudson River* and got everyone off safely? And yes, for a while in early adulthood especially, the real world of politics seemed to provide me with some examples of greatness, though I admit that more recently I have tended to adopt the advice of the psalmist: "Put not your trust in princes."

The proximate cause of trying to reflect systematically on my hodgepodge of heroes—and more broadly on what heroism is—was a Thanksgiving dinner at my in-laws in New Jersey. As usual, and arriving late as usual, my wife's Uncle David, an Ocean Township police officer, was there. But he had recently done a remarkable thing: He'd run into a burning building to rescue a child from the fire. You'll read a little more about him in Chapter 8.

Uncle David didn't necessarily seem the heroic type: a good-looking ladies' man of self-confident charm, for sure, but heroic? Yet there he was, and it turned out this was not his first such outing: In his youth, working as a lifeguard, he'd had occasion to save someone from drowning. That was two notches for him in a belt most people never try to put on. A couple years later came 9/11 and the unforgettable display of the ultimate form of heroism by so many New York City firefighters—and subsequently, a new chapter in the heroism of the American soldier.

Thus we arrive at the heart of our inquiry in the pages that follow: A hero is someone with a claim to some kind of superiority. The modern world writ large, wherever it exists on the globe today, is democratic and egalitarian, a sensibility that has thoroughly taken hold among its residents, including ourselves. What kind of claim of superiority or greatness, then, is compatible with the modern world's democratic and egalitarian character?

To fully appreciate the defining characteristics of heroism in the modern world, it's necessary to look as well at some of the heroic or great characters who inhabited the world prior to the spread of the spirit of democracy and equality. To understand the heroic element of Uncle David in the context of his times, we need to understand the heroic element of King David in the context of his. Because let's face it: Although the 9/11 firefighter's heroism fits in just fine with the modern world, we really have no place for Achilles these days. Indeed, Brad Pitt in the movie *Troy* notwithstanding, Achilles today often comes across as a preeningly self-centered brat. As to why Homer would write an epic poem about a narcissist with delusions of grandeur when his adversary Hector seems like the better man, well, that's a good question.

But the reason it's a good question is that we really need to examine the set of prejudices—*modern* prejudices—that lead us, if they do, to a dismissive view of the greatness of Achilles. Homer takes the heroic heart of Achilles seriously. So should we—and we will in the pages that follow.

From the influence the modern, democratic, egalitarian perspective has on views of heroism, we can see that the story of heroism also turns into a story about politics—specifically, about the relationship between the heroic type, whether it's Achilles or a 9/11 firefighter, and political order and change. This, too, is a subject of our inquiry here.

I should make clear at the beginning that though we will be considering "greatness ancient and modern," this investigation is not a *history*, in which a new view of greatness or heroism emerges in the world to grapple with and take over for an older view of heroic achievement. On the contrary, as we shall see, the type of greatness honored in the modern world has deep roots in antiquity. Nor is it so certain, on closer examination, that the modern world has rid itself once and for all of the classically heroic type.

By the end of this book, I hope you will find the latter prospect just as ominous as I do.

## CHAPTER 1

# GODS AND HEROES

*The origins of heroism. Immortals and mortals,*
*the willingness to risk death,*
*inner greatness.*

The three biggest things human beings have in common are life, death, and the consciousness of both, including the ability to speak with each other about all three. Nonhuman animals may possess intelligence and self-awareness; the will to keep living or "survival instinct" may be as strong in them as in any person. But they can't talk among themselves about what life and death mean. That conversation is the start of our story.

Who am I? How did I get here? Who are these others? What do they want? What do I want? What *should* I want? These are primal questions. We would do a grave injustice to our ancestors to presume that because we have more knowledge of biological and social processes than they, their grappling with exactly the same questions was any less profound than ours.

A phrase often attributed to Aristotle to describe human beings is *zoon logon echon*. The phrase is often translated as "rational animal," following a detour from the ancient Greek to English by way of Latin. A more direct rendering is "the animal that talks." That leaves us as heirs to and custodians of a set of questions about who we are and how we should live—something we do indeed have the capacity to talk about—without necessarily granting us the capacity to arrive at a final, "rational" answer we must all agree to.

"The animal that talks" takes us in the right direction: language is a shared understanding that enables, through interchange, further and deeper shared understanding. Of course language also allows for the expression of disagreement, and may at times even contribute to disagreement, as terms get confused and people harden their positions in opposition to each other—to say nothing of the possibility of lying. Disagreement is prior to language, even if language often expresses disagreement and leads to new disagreements. But language is also a means to bridge disagreement.

Where did language come from? The answer common to the ancient world was: from God, or the gods. Interestingly, the matter that seems most to have vexed our forebears, according to the texts and traditions that have come down to us, was the multiplicity of languages. In many accounts, all people originally spoke the same language—until a deity intervened, dividing tribe from tribe by means of language. The implication is that the ability to speak with one another was once a common property of all human beings. A world in which people are divided one from another by language therefore represents a falling away from a better prior condition.

In the ancient understanding, human beings are not only created in the image of God, as the Genesis account and many others hold. They also speak the language of God or the gods, an understanding that does not seem to have struck our forebears as especially noteworthy at the time. In the ancient world, there appears not to have been much additional curiosity about the initial human acquisition of language. The doings of the gods were explanation enough. There would have been no need, prior to Darwin, for an account of how human beings *became* the animals that talk. The stories about God (or the gods) giving speech to human beings, or simply talking to a comprehending human being, were sufficient explanation.

We, who do not accept as literally true the biblical or mythological accounts of creation and the speech that comes to human beings along with it, need a little more detail in the account of the origin of speech, and thus the *dawn* of the human. Yet we can have no direct access to the origin or invention of speech. Even stories about humans brought up without speech—say, the feral child of myth and story (Tarzan, Mowgli) and, alas, occasionally reality (Danielle Crockett, a seven-year-old girl found stashed away in a Florida basement in 2005)—take place in a world in which others can speak. There is no going back. Our only recourse is speculation.

At the origin of speech must have been a terrible struggle to say anything at all and make it understood. In the Genesis account (2:19–20), God puts the animals He has created before Adam to see what Adam will call them. Thus the animals get their names. A conventional interpretation here is that God thereby grants man the power to create language. That can't be quite right, however, because God has already spoken to the man (2:16), telling him to feel free to eat the fruit of any tree but one. On the other hand, the imputation to man of the naming power does at least gesture toward a world in which things have no names—in which man is not yet but is about to become the animal who talks, by his own labor. And emphatically, the naming is associated with a grant of power: God has given man dominion over the plants and animals.

Yet in the absence of a benevolent god to speed the process along, it is hard to imagine the origin of language as anything but an epic struggle taking place in the context of a *preverbal* epic struggle—for simple survival for oneself and for the band of primate protohumans in which one found oneself, and for dominance within that band. Who knows what kind of force might (or must) have accompanied the first-ever assertion, "Mine!"? In the grunt of the caveman lies the origin of property and the demand for recognition, or justice. Perhaps we have cavewomen to thank for the first discourse unconnected to the sheer assertion of power.

With language comes a quantum leap in the power of imagination—envisioning the world around us as something different from what it is.

Imagination is surely preverbal: perhaps cavepeople sometimes dreamt they could fly and remembered the dreams when they woke up. Surely such a dream would color one's impression the next time one observed a bird in flight. But language offers a more comprehensive possibility for the imagination.

Behold the corpse of a member of your cave clan, alive yesterday, dead today. When there is no possibility of saying anything about this brute fact, it's hard to see how the imaginative capacity could extend much beyond recalling the corpse as a living being and projecting that image forward in contrast to the dead thing at hand. This might produce sadness or grief at the loss (or, depending on one's relations with the recently departed, it might produce memories of fear and a sense of relief). One might also look at the living and imagine them dead, with similar effects on one's mood.

A preverbal curiosity about what exactly happened to the living element of the now-dead seems inescapable. And indeed, here we are but one step away from the birth of metaphysics. But it's hard to see how such postulates as the immortality of the soul and the contours of the afterlife would come up in the absence of the ability to talk the problem over. The development of increasingly sophisticated language was certainly a useful tool in everyday life for the cave clan. But for the purpose of speculation about the meaning of life and death, it was absolutely essential. "In the beginning was the Word": well, yes.

In accounting for the development and spread of language, we moderns, being of a generally utilitarian cast of mind, are probably inclined to emphasize the practical utility of language to the cave clan—its productivity-enhancing element in the cave. No doubt the efficiency of both hunting and gathering improved with the development of language.

But we should at least entertain the possibility that the bigger impetus to speech was the necessity of language to cave clan metaphysics. There were certain facts available to preverbal protohumans that really did call out for a deeper shared understanding, life and death first among them.

Because language to grapple with these facts did not exist, it was necessary to invent it.

Speculative anthropology—including speculation about the anthropogenic moment, the point at which hominids became human—is a risky and necessarily inconclusive business. But it is likely fair to conclude that at some distant prehistoric point in the gazing of the living upon the newly dead, it first occurred to human beings to imagine beings somewhat like themselves but different in one decisive respect: they would not die. They would be immortal. And with this quality, these speculative beings would have a vast, inestimable superiority to the mortal beings speculating about them. The mortals would have to invent a new name to distinguish beings of this kind from themselves. They would have this need for a name quite apart from the question of whether such immortal beings actually exist or had made their existence manifest to mortals. "Gods" would do.

I take no position here on whether God created man in His image, or for that matter whether a superior and divine power called "God" or anything else was in fact responsible for the creation of human beings by whatever means. I would only note that prior to the anthropogenic moment and the human acquisition of language, any revelation by God or the gods of His or their existence would have fallen on, so to speak, deaf ears. There would have been no capacity to process the revelation, or to develop a shared understanding of it with others.

Of course, if God created man precisely in the manner described in Genesis, with language present at the creation, then God would have had no trouble making His presence known and significance understood. Speculative anthropology in that case would be pointless.

But it is not pointless. Another way of looking at the Genesis account is that in starting with a human being in possession of language, it begins where revelation of the existence of God would first be intelligible to man. To continue the quotation from John, "In the beginning was the Word, and the Word was with God, and the Word was God." The validity of this statement in anthropogenic terms is not dependent on its theological truth: With the language hominids acquired in the course of becoming human, they could for the first time imagine and exchange views on a type of being like them in possession of language, but different in not having to die. They would be driven to it by the experience of their own lives and the death of others. They would recognize this immortal being as superior to their own being, and because superior, possibly in possession of additional powers—up to and including the power to create and destroy them.

In their search for explanations for the workings of the world around them, some would perceive the influence of these additional, divine powers: the busyness of the gods in the rising of the sun, the flowing of a river, the change of the seasons, the variability of the weather. Some would long for and seek the intercession of the power of the superior being in pursuit of good things (say, a successful hunt) and to prevent bad things (say, a drought). Others might conclude that such a divine being was not real, but rather entirely imaginary—a point of view that, should it be expressed, might call forth the wrath of believers worried about the reaction of the superior being to the presence of unbelief among mere mortals. It's only the degree of severity of a potential angry reaction to disbelief that distinguishes these prehistoric debates from those taking place in the modern world on precisely the same subject.

Whether God is in his Heaven or not, human beings from the beginning of "the Word" have been moved to contemplate their own mortality in contrast to the prospect of eternal life. Much of the speculation, of course, has centered on whether death is really the end, and if it is not, what happens afterward. The prospect of a benevolent eternity of life has long beguiled people, although it has often been accompanied by the anxiety that eternity will be a torment. What, if anything, one can do while alive on Earth to influence the outcome favorably has also been a subject of intense interest. But we start with human beings in a tragic position: Almost from the very moment at which they can say to each other, "We are alive," they long for a permanency to life they cannot have—except, perhaps, through death, though here the afterlife remains entirely a speculative affair. Life without death is a primal longing of mortal being.

Human beings have developed an extraordinary array of strategies for coping with this unattainable longing. They have developed religious faith, or, if you prefer, they have accepted the truth of religion on the basis of revelation. Most religions promise that earthly mortality is not the end. The immortal soul goes on to another plane of being, or perhaps awaits reincarnation in a new body.

Some have tried philosophy: The Roman statesman and orator Marcus Tullius Cicero called the "whole life of a philosopher . . . a meditation on death," which the philosopher Montaigne took to be the exercise of "learn[ing] to die." Perhaps the consolation of philosophy is individual possession of eternal truth, or an awareness of what it means to long for such truth. Perhaps it is the pleasure of membership in an elite community of those, living or dead, now and to come, who know the truth.

Some make art that will outlast them. No one will ever know what got into the heads of the people who made the first cave paintings, which date back more than 30,000 years in Europe. Maybe the paintings were merely an ephemeral effort to spruce up the cave. Maybe, on the other hand, the desire to leave a permanent mark was part of the motivation. If so, the fact that the paintings can strike wonder in the minds of those living 1,200 generations later constitutes vindication. The desire of those ancient cave painters may be the same desire that motivates some of the artists of our day.

A small number seek by earthly deeds to win glory—not only the acclaim of human beings of their time, but also of generations to come as their stories are told and retold. The path to glory might entail conquering the world or exploring its unknown reaches. It might also be the pursuit of great scientific discoveries or sports triumphs.

On a more mundane level, people have children and grandchildren, and they often see a piece of themselves as living on through their descendants. They took this view long before the development of knowledge of genetics enabled us to think in terms of passing our genes along. Of course, we ourselves had our genes passed along to us, all the way back to the primordial soup, so perhaps we ourselves are merely temporary embodiments of a gene pool that preceded us and will extend itself indefinitely into the future; the human species, if not life itself, can become the vehicle for the contemplation of a type of immortality for each of its members.

Denial is also an option. One can just try to live out the life one has while giving as little thought to death as possible. In the state of nature as Thomas Hobbes imagined it, the "worst of all" elements of the human condition was "continual fear of violent death." He detected three passions that "incline men to peace": "fear of death, desire of such things as are necessary to commodious living, and a hope by their industry to obtain them." The state of nature includes a primal vision of a quiet and comfortable life, as well as the acknowledgment that such quietude and comfort are not natural; they have to be created by human "industry." Such industry would include not only performing the work necessary to secure one's daily bread, but also the work involved in creating and sustaining a state with a government strong enough to secure liberation from the "war of every man against every man."

The modern, developed world, has come a long way from the Hobbesian state of nature. For those lucky enough to be born into it, unlike for the vast majority of human beings who have come before and for most of those alive now, life can be quite pleasant, what with evenings and weekends off, the Internet, cable, sporting events and concerts, and decent food available year-round. In the Sermon on the Mount, Matthew quotes Jesus admonishing his listeners: "So do not worry about tomorrow; for tomorrow will care for itself. Each day has enough trouble of its own" (Matthew 6:34). So it did; coping with the here and now was a challenge sufficient to keep most people fully occupied. The message of modernity is not to worry about tomorrow because each day brings *pleasures* of its own. And who can doubt that people born in pre-modern circumstances today, at least those seeking chiefly a quiet life for themselves, would switch places in a heartbeat to rid themselves of as much daily trouble as they could?

Unfortunately, none of these strategies for dealing with mortality—from religion's promise of life after death, to philosophy's contemplation of the eternal, to the creation of something meant to last, to the pursuit of glory, to one's sense of place in the passing of the generations, to the urge to change the subject—has had the effect of actually eliminating physical death. And it is at this dead-end, so to speak, where we first encounter the subject of our study, the hero. The first thing that distinguishes heroes from the unheroic vast majority of human beings is a very different attitude from most others on the subject of mortality, starting with their own.

Heroes seek, by actions risking their lives, to demonstrate that death has no power over them. Their greatness will out, come what may. As Lord Krishna advises the warrior-king Arjuna on the eve of a great battle: "Be intent on action. / not on the fruits of action; / avoid attachment to the fruits"—including even the personal life-or-death consequences of action.

It's not that heroes are under the illusion that they won't themselves die. Homer's Achilles, the greatest hero of the classical world, was thoroughly imbued with this sense of his own mortality. Though the son of the immortal goddess Thetis, Achilles was not exempted from the mortality of his father Peleus, the great king of the Myrmidons.

The "continual fear of violent death" that Hobbes identified as the worst aspect of the human condition is something a hero such as Achilles overcomes. A hero doesn't seek death, but neither does a hero let the possibility of violent death deter resolute action toward the purpose at hand. Of those who are so deterred, one may say that death has a power over them even as they live. The fear of death shapes their responses to the events of their lives. The prospect of putting oneself at *additional* risk of untimely and violent death is simply abhorrent, a non-starter: one would ordinarily run in the opposite direction from such a risk. The response to the sudden perception of danger, or fear, has long been known to produce a physiological response in humans and other animals: a higher pulse rate and a surge of adrenaline, which enhances perception and concentration. The so-called "fight-or-flight" response (some add "freeze" as a third option) kicks in *in extremis*. But the heroic type has this response firmly in hand: neither freezing nor running away in terror is an option. Action in accordance with their own sense of inner greatness or virtue is a must. "To be great," as Rousseau wrote, "it is necessary only to become master of oneself."

In the Greek word of Homer's day, the heroic warrior's response is *aristeia*, "a victorious rampage, irresistibly sweeping all before him, killing whomever of the enemy he can catch or whoever stands against him." The combat, moreover, was intimate and hand-to-hand, conducted with spear and sword and club. The connection between combatants at the moment at which one prevails and the other succumbs was human at its most brutal, as in Achilles rushing into the Trojan ranks in Book XX of the *Iliad*:

> . . . his first kill was Iphition,
> Otrynteus' hardy son and a chief of large contingents. . . .
> As the Trojan charged head-on Achilles speared him
> Square in the brows—his whole skull split in half
> And down he crashed, Achilles exulting over him:
> "Here you lie, Otrynteus' son—most terrible man alive!
> Here's your deathbed! . . ." (XX 436–444)

There is no advance guarantee that one's rampage will be victorious; charging headlong into battle courts death. Iphition, too, charged into the fight: He was sufficiently formidable in his own right and by family heritage for Achilles to recognize him as he perished. The *Iliad* is not Iphition's tale; he appears in it only to die in this passage. But neither does the *Iliad* depict the death of Achilles himself. Though much foretold throughout, and well understood to be ineluctably forthcoming by audiences from Homer's day to our own, Achilles's death takes place after the conclusion of the *Iliad*, whose final concern is the return to Troy of the body of Achilles's last victim, Hector, the beloved son of Troy's King Priam. Heroes—and Iphition perhaps lacked only an epic chronicle of his own for us to regard him as one—not only risk death but sometimes do actually die in battle.

Here, perhaps, the question is how they die: As Hector and Achilles begin their final confrontation, Hector realizes that the gods have turned their backs on him:

> "So now I meet my doom. Well let me die—
> but not without struggle, not without glory, no,
> in some great clash of arms that even men to come
> will hear of down the years!" (XXII 359–362)

Hector gets his wish, of course: We still pay attention to his epic clash with Achilles, and it still has something to teach us.

Hector's willingness to engage in a struggle worthy of his high sense of himself, though not unique to the victorious hero Achilles, was hardly universal among the combatants. Homer narrates one such case that stands in sharp contrast:

> . . . Tros, Alastor's son, crawled to Achilles' knees
> and clutched them, hoping he'd spare him,
> let Tros off alive. . . .
> Here was a man [Achilles, that is] not sweet at heart, not kind, no,
> he was raging, wild—as Tros grasped his knees,
> desperate, begging, Achilles slit open his liver,
> the liver spurted loose, gushing with dark blood,
> drenched his lap and the night swirled down his eyes
> as his life breath slipped away. (XX 523–533)

When the Trojan prince Aegnor sees Achilles coming, he considers trying to run for it, but rejects the idea when he realizes Achilles will "catch me and slash my coward's throat." Then he considers hiding out, but worries lest Achilles "sees me turning tail." Aegnor fears death less than he fears ignominy.

The distinctive characteristic of the heroic figure is the willingness to risk death. It may be done in ignorance of the outcome, as in the case of Iphition, and therefore with the hope of success foremost in the mind up until the very end. It may be subject to post facto regret, as in the case of poor Tros, abjectly unheroic in the final scene of his life. It may be a matter of weighing alternatives and dismissing as inferior all but standing one's ground, as for Aegnor. And it may be that the decision to risk violent death is subject to reversal as circumstances develop; Homer says the god Apollo arranged for Aegnor to make a getaway. But what matters in the first instance is the pursuit of *aristeia*, the mantle of the victorious warrior.

There are a number of qualities that set Achilles apart as a hero above and beyond the other greats of the ancient world. He is, by universal acknowledgment of his peers, the greatest of the Achaean warriors. He has an unusual capacity for self-understanding, even in the midst of his passion. And above all, unlike any other mortal, Achilles knows in advance what the outcome of his decision to stay at Troy will be:

> "[. . .] Mother tells me,
> the immortal goddess Thetis with her glistening feet,
> that two fates bear me on to the day of death.
> If I hold out here and I lay siege to Troy,
> my journey home is gone, but my glory never dies.
> If I voyage back to the fatherland I love,
> my pride, my glory dies . . .
> true, but the life that's left me will be long,
> the stroke of death will not come on quickly." (IX 497–505)

Achilles is acutely aware of the consequences of the choice before him. To stay and fight does not merely allow for the *possibility* of dying young—that is, one possibility among others, including the possibility of winning eternal glory in battle *and* returning home to a long and happy life. For Achilles, an untimely demise is a certainty if he stays and fights. No doubt many of the Achaeans besieging Troy set out from their homes well aware that they might not return. But they could *hope* for a victory that would cover them in glory, and *hope* as well to return home to a long and happy life. In fact, that hope might abide within them up to the very moment of death. Some, like Tros, realizing that the enterprise was going to end badly, ended up regretting the whole thing. In pleading for his life, Tros forfeits a heroic profile in favor of keeping hope alive a moment longer. The hope that everything turns out well in the end is, in most instances of heroic action then and now, one of the spurs to the willingness to put one's life at greater risk. But there is no hope underlying the actions of Achilles. He knows his fate in advance. If he stays in Troy, it's death and glory. One could fairly describe the story of the *Iliad* as Achilles coming to terms with his own superiority and mortality.

Homer advises us, from the first word of the first sentence of the *Iliad*, that the subject matter of the poem is the "rage" or "wrath" of Achilles. Throughout the poem, Achilles burns. His rage has two divisions, each encompassing roughly half the *Iliad*. The first object of Achilles's rage is the Achaean king, Agamemnon. We will turn to it in the next chapter, when the time comes to try to understand more fully the political problem that heroes pose. Here, we skip to the second source of Achilles's rage: the death of Achilles's comrade-in-arms and confidant, Patroclus, in battle at the hand of Hector, son of the Trojan king.

The relationship between Achilles and Patroclus is somewhat mysterious. The depth of Achilles's attachment to his friend is something Homer asserts and reveals the consequences of, but does not explore. It lacks what T.S. Eliot, writing about *Hamlet*, called an "objective correlative": As Hamlet's extreme emotional responses seem excessive relative to the facts as presented in the play, so too does Achilles's response to his friend's death seem extreme relative to what we know about them. Homer does not show us how the bond between the two formed or much of how it operated in the nine years of the Trojan War prior to the beginning of the *Iliad*.

The old king Nestor, who recruited Achilles and Patroclus to Agamemnon's cause in the war, recalls Patroclus's father telling him to give Achilles "sound advice, guide him, even in battle" (XI 941). Patroclus, for his part, is evidently comfortable with the characterization of himself as advice-giver to Achilles. Yet through this point in the *Iliad*, there is no scene in which we see Patroclus actually offering Achilles advice. In fact, apart from hanging out in the company of Achilles—that is, simply being there—what we see Patroclus doing is exactly what Achilles tells him to do.

Patroclus is older than Achilles—a detail that runs somewhat counter to the impression of Patroclus as more or less Achilles's pet. In their youth, Patroclus perhaps played the role of an older brother to Achilles: role model and sparring partner. Yet there is no lingering trace of such a role depicted in the *Iliad*. Later Greeks and modern critics alike have speculated about a homoerotic attachment as an explanation for the depth of Achilles's sentiment, notwithstanding the absence of a direct textual basis for such a conclusion.

What we have in Patroclus, in the end, is the slightly older best friend and amiable constant companion to a man superior to himself in all respects, but evidently not above the need or desire or wish for such companionship and friendship: Even a great hero, "best of the Achaeans," wants a great friend.

Why Patroclus? We still know little. It's possible that in the *Iliad* (in *Hamlet* as well, for that matter), the absence of the objective correlative for great emotion—notwithstanding Eliot's judgment of artistic failure—is a deliberate attempt on the part of the author to draw our attention to something. *We do not ultimately know* why Achilles is so attached to Patroclus. Achilles may or may not himself be able to articulate an explanation, let alone one we would find adequate. We confront, therefore, the bare fact of the greatest warrior's greatest friend, and we must not rationalize it or explain it away, but take it seriously on its own terms.

It's not until Patroclus is dead at the hand of Hector that Achilles definitively chooses to stay at Troy, thus exposing himself to the inevitability of dying young in accordance with the second of the two possible paths before him. Achilles laments to his mother:

> . . . "My dear comrade's dead—
> Patroclus—the man I loved beyond all other comrades,
> loved as my own life—I've lost him— . . .
> . . . the dearest life I know." (XVIII 94–96, 136)

To put it perfectly bluntly, if Achilles, the greatest warrior, says Patroclus is worth the sacrifice of the life of the greatest warrior—not even to *save* Patroclus, mind you, but simply to avenge his death—then who are you to disagree? Achilles does not owe you an account. He, "great in his greatness," has made his decision.

Patroclus gets himself killed as a result of a scheme to try to draw Achilles out of his tent, where he has been brooding over Agamemnon's slight, and back into the fight, which has been going badly in his absence. Patroclus, Achilles has agreed, will lead the Myrmidon army into battle wearing Achilles's armor. But Achilles has admonished Patroclus that if the tide of battle turns in their favor, Patroclus must not pursue the retreating Trojans back to their city walls. Achilles frankly tells Patroclus that if Patroclus advances on Troy without him, "You will only make *my* glory that much less . . ." (XVI 105). The terms of the friendship between Achilles and Patroclus belong to Achilles to set.

Addressing Patroclus on the eve of battle, he concludes his speech with an appeal to the gods that is extraordinarily apocalyptic:

"not one of these Trojans could flee his death, not one,

no Argive either, but we [Achilles and Patroclus] could stride from
   the slaughter

so we could bring Troy's hallowed crown of towers

toppling down around us—you and I alone!" (XVI 116–119)

The chilling vision Achilles conjures is of himself and his comrade the conquering sole survivors striding out of fields of the Trojan and Argive dead (Achilles and Patroclus are Myrmidons, not Argives). Achilles has spoken of his honor and glory as things he values highly, and he has absented himself from battle because of an insult. But there is no acclaim to be discerned in his fantasy-vision here; no one is left to take in the destruction of Troy but Patroclus and himself. It is not for the acclaim of the Achaeans that Achilles will fight, but for himself, with his comrade at his side. Achilles proffers a vision of a perfected glory, enjoyed solely by himself and his friend, that requires nothing of others. The dead have no opinions. Achilles and his friend are ultimately the only ones worthy of apprehending the greatness of Achilles—and Patroclus for no reason other than that *Achilles* has chosen him. Everyone else is expendable.

The rampaging Patroclus does indeed succeed in turning back the Trojan attack. But he continues to advance on Troy. He does not do as Achilles told him. And he dies at the hand of Hector. His last words are of Achilles, an admonition to Hector that Achilles will cut Hector down in turn. Patroclus believes his own death will bring Achilles into the battle. He is right.

Achilles, back in his tent, is full of foreboding. He has seen the tide of battle turn twice: first, against the Trojans, at the eleventh hour, as they were on the verge of burning the Argive ships, thanks presumably to Patroclus; now, alarmingly, back against the Achaeans.

Moments later, when word arrives that his fears are justified, Achilles is devastated. Homer depicts him befouling himself with dirt and ash, pulling out his hair, weeping, crying out in anguish. Achilles is tops in grief as well. His mother the goddess comes to him, and he tells her that she too will know "unending sorrows" (XVIII 102), for he is determined to kill Hector—setting in motion the course that will inevitably result, by the prophecy, in Achilles dying young.

The apocalyptic vision Achilles proffered—he and Patroclus alone standing among the Argive and Trojan dead as the towers of Troy crumble—is now impossible. With Patroclus dead, Achilles's affinity for the human is gone. His grievance with Agamemnon is now meaningless. Achilles desires only two things of the human world: First, he wants revenge, which he will soon exact in his climactic rampage by the pitiless killing of Trojan warriors, culminating in his pursuit of Hector, Hector's death at his hands, and the desecration of Hector's corpse, which Achilles takes back with him to the Myrmidon camp. Second, since he knows he will soon die, he wants his bones buried with those of Patroclus, for whom he has arranged an elaborate funeral, including the ghastly slaughter of twelve captive Trojans next to the pyre. Once he avenges Patroclus, it is only his mortality that continues to bind him to the human world.

Priam, the Trojan king, steals into the Myrmidon camp to beg for the return of his son's body to mount a proper funeral. Achilles agrees, expressing some sympathy for the Trojan king's loss. But it is not the human quality of the appeal from Priam that is decisive in persuading Achilles to give back the body. Rather, it is because Zeus himself has made clear to Achilles that the god-king himself wants Achilles to return Hector's body to Priam. A request grounded in common human affinity would mean nothing to Achilles by this point. But when a god asks something of him, he can respond as a peer.

Though the *Iliad* concludes with the Trojans burying Hector, Homer is not altogether done with Achilles. He turns up again in the *Odyssey*, the story of the wily Ithacan king Odysseus's complicated journey home following the sack of Troy. Odysseus spins a tale about a visit he paid to the underworld, where he encounters (among others) the shades of a number of illustrious figures from the Trojan War.

Circe, a goddess with whom Odysseus has been shacking up for a year, has directed Odysseus to go to the underworld to consult on his destiny with the ghost of Tiresias, the great seer of Thebes. Odysseus is to make a blood sacrifice; once Tiresias and the other shades drink from it, they will be able to talk to him. Circe describes Tiresias as "the great blind prophet whose mind remains unshaken" (X 542) even after death. He is unique in this regard. She notes chillingly, "The rest of the dead are empty, flitting shades" (X 545).

The underworld is a deeply ambiguous place in Homer's telling. On one hand, there *is* an afterlife, a place the souls of mortals go when they die, and where they continue in perpetuity. Death is not the end. On the other, the existence of these ghosts is something other than and distinctly less than human. The underworld is not Hell, exactly, but it is certainly not Heaven.

Before he meets Achilles, Odysseus encounters his great comrade Agamemnon:

> "He knew me at once, as soon as he drank the blood,
> and wailed out, shrilly; tears sprang to his eyes,
> he thrust his arms toward me, keen to embrace me there—
> no use—the great force was gone, the strength lost forever,
> now, that filled his rippling limbs in the old days." (X 443–447)

The physicality that was Agamemnon, the power of his person, is no more. So is the capability of embracing a comrade. The bodily aspect of the human is essential to the fullness of human experience. Though the joy produced by meeting an old friend is a mental state, and Agamemnon's shade feels it powerfully enough to bring tears to his eyes, without the bodily element of the embrace, the joy is incompletely realized. The result is ineffably sad.

And this is *after* Agamemnon drinks the blood, which has brought him back to a kind of life, at least in the sense of the ability to interact with a living human. In the absence of Achilles's sacrifice, he is just another of the "empty, flitting shades." Here, Homer powerfully evokes the superiority of life to the eternal afterlife of the underworld.

There are, of course, beings in the *Iliad* and the *Odyssey* who possess both eternal life and physicality. They are the gods. Their power is even greater than the "great force" of the living Agamemnon. They eat and drink and love and lust like humans—and never have to face the prospect of the end. Achilles became like them through force of inner greatness—the ability of a great hero to overcome the power of death by his willingness to risk dying. In the case of Achilles, it was not merely a risk: it was a certainty, thanks to the prophecy. Death had no more power over him while he lived than it does over the eternal gods.

But Achilles did die. A hero is not a god, no matter how god-like. And what does Achilles think of his disembodied eternal life in the underworld? Odysseus ventures some speculation directly to his old comrade:

> "there's not a man in the world more blest than you—
> there never has been, never will be one.
> Time was, when you were alive, we Argives
> honored you as a god, and now down here, I see,
> you lord it over the dead in all your power.
> So grieve no more at dying, great Achilles." (X 548–553)

Achilles will have none of this:

> "No winning words about death to *me*, shining Odysseus!
> By god, I'd rather slave on earth for another man—
> some dirt-poor tenant farmer who scrapes to keep alive—
> than rule down here over all the breathless dead." (X 555–558)

As Achilles describes those who dwell in the "House of Death," they are "the senseless, burnt-out wraiths of mortals" (X 539–540).

The great Achilles feels no greatness in death. He says he would prefer life as the lowest sort of person he can imagine to his incorporeal existence in the underworld. What has become of the inner greatness of Achilles, that he should compare himself unfavorably to a *serf*?

The answer is that he is no longer able to live life in such a fashion as to risk death. There is no exit from the House of Death: nothing to fear, nothing to hope for. In the underworld, his heroic heart has been deprived of the only condition in which it can flourish, that of mortal man.

But suppose Achilles had become a god? Though it never happens the other way around, conversion from mortal to immortal was not without precedent in Zeus's world. This, alas, would not solve the problem. Death being an impossibility for an immortal, the gods are likewise incapable of risking death. Insofar as greatness of the kind Achilles embodied entails the willingness to risk one's life, the gods are incapable of it. Death is something whose power they never have occasion to overcome. Next to the living Achilles, the gods seem childlike, innocent in their ignorance of the full meaning for living mortals of both death and greatness.

The underworld of "the breathless dead" is apparently completely cut off from the world of living humans, except under such extraordinary circumstances as those of Odysseus (and Heracles, another great hero, one of whose challenges was to descend to the underworld and bring back Cerberus, its three-headed guard dog). So Achilles then asks Odysseus for news of his son, Neoptolemus, and his old father. When I think about it, it's exactly the question I would put to a visitor from the world of the living if I had made an untimely exit eighteen years ago to an underworld resembling that of the Greeks: How's my family, how are my children? There is nothing at all heroic about Achilles's inquiry. Indeed, it is a perfect expression of his journey in death to the realm of the ordinary. Death is an equalizer, visiting the heroic and the ordinary alike.

Odysseus tells Achilles that Neoptolemus is thriving, a fearless terror in battle and unscathed from it.

> "So I said and
> off he [Achilles] went, the ghost of the great runner, Aecus' grandson
> loping with long strides across the fields of asphodel
> triumphant in all I had told him about his son,
> his gallant, glorious son." (X 612–616)

Achilles is at last happy in death, because he is thinking not about himself and the condition to which his greatness has been reduced, but of his son doing well in the world of the living.

So a funny thing happened around the time of the birth of metaphysics in the cave clan. Mortal human beings tried to postulate a kind of being, immortal being, superior to their mortal being in being relieved of the necessity to die. And they succeeded, only to reveal that a certain human type, the hero willing to risk death, in so doing reaches a higher place than an immortal could in all eternity.

## CHAPTER 2

# THE DANGER OF HEROES

*The inevitable collision of heroic types
with politics. The instability of political order
in the age of classical heroism.*

What most distinguishes the politics of the ancient world from the politics of the modern world is that political failure in the ancient world was routinely a matter of life and death. The rewards for success in politics were and are great, now as then: acclaim, riches, the freedom to associate with the similarly high and mighty. The penalty for failure, however, is now much diminished. If you lose an election or make a bad decision these days, you do not typically lose your head.

Consider the case of the Greek city-state of Melos in the fifth century BCE. As Thucydides describes it in the *History of the Peloponnesian War*, all the Melians wanted was to remain neutral in the war between Athens and Sparta. But that wasn't good enough for the Athenians, who demanded Melos's allegiance as well as annual tribute. A delegation of blunt-speaking Athenian generals visited Melos and met with some of its leading citizens, explaining in no uncertain terms that in case of noncompliance, Athens would destroy Melos. The Melians, for centuries a proud and independent people, refused to bend to the Athenian demands.

They voiced their conviction that because Melos was a colony of Sparta, if Athens attacked the Spartans would come to their aid. In any case, the Melians said, they believed they would prevail because the gods knew their cause was just. The Athenians scoffed at Melian naïveté.

The Athenians turned out to be right: The Spartans didn't come to the Melians' rescue. Nor did the gods. So to punish the Melian defiance, after defeating them in battle, the Athenians killed every last one of the men of Melos and sold all the women and children into slavery. Now there was a political decision with consequences.

Or consider the problem of the danger of politics from the point of view not of a weak city-state but of a powerful tyrant: Many and various are the people who might like to kill you and become tyrant themselves. In a wry dialogue composed by Plato's contemporary Xenophon, *Hiero* or *Tyrannicus*, Hiero the tyrant paints an elaborate portrait of himself and his fellow tyrants as the most miserable of all human beings, each a de facto prisoner of his absolute power. True, he gets the most pleasing spectacles, the best food, the sweetest words of praise, sex with the loveliest boy. But these are only sources of misery to him, since a common man can travel freely to see a variety of spectacles in a way that no tyrant can; and since the best food, eaten every day, becomes a bore; and since the praise he receives all comes from flatterers; and since the boy will never really love him. Hiero laments that though tyrants "are acquainted with the decent, the wise, and the just," they "fear rather than admire them. They fear the brave because they might dare something for the sake of their freedom; the wise, because they might contrive something; and the just, because the multitude might desire to be ruled by them. When, because of their fear, they do away secretly with such men, who is left for them to use save the unjust, the incontinent, and the slavish?" (5:1–2). It takes a certain sense of self to kill off all the best people around you and then complain that there is no one left worth your time.

Why, then, go into politics at all? Or why not try get out of it? Why not seek a quiet private life instead? Perhaps the questions are anachronistic—in the sense that we modern types have drunk deeply of the primal human desire Hobbes described, that for a quiet life. Hiero clearly believes he has no choice but to continue as tyrant, because he has made so many enemies who would be only too happy to do him in if ever he did give up the power he wields. This concern seems just as applicable to modern-day tyrants, even if tyranny is less prevalent these days.

But missing from Hiero's account of himself, and deliberately so, is any kind of acknowledgment of the chief benefit, indeed joy, of being tyrant. It's that nobody, but nobody, can tell you what to do. You are free in the most basic sense of the term, free of the compulsory authority of all others. Nature still constrains you, of course; you remain mortal. But your fellow human beings do not constrain you. There may be other nearby tyrants who would like to add to what they have everything you have, and you may have to fight them—to conquer or be conquered. You may have to take special measures to protect yourself. But within the sphere of your authority, it is absolute.

Hiero seems to understand the utterly arbitrary nature of the power he wields: He makes no claim to *deserve* to rule beyond the indisputable political fact that he does rule. He might well readily grant that if someone managed to successfully challenge his power, then that person would deserve to rule no less (and no more) than he himself does. The Athenian generals visiting Melos captured this sentiment rather ably: "Of the gods we believe, and of men we know, that by a necessary law of their nature they rule wherever they can." The operative word is "can." Not, "wherever they want to," implying discretionary latitude about whether to rule; but "wherever they can," a pure test of strength. This is a vision of politics bereft of all considerations of justice or morality: absolute power creating absolute rule, which entails absolute discretion on all questions but one: whether to exercise the absolute power.

But not all rulers are tyrants. Some who possess power that may verge on the absolute also possess something else, namely legitimacy in one form or another. This is the point at which a ruler becomes not a tyrant but a king. In the next chapter, we will have a chance to look at heroic kings and heroes who go on to set themselves up as kings, by founding either a state or something equally noteworthy, or by taking one over. For now, however, we need to examine what happens when a king or other ruler whose legitimacy is widely accepted runs into someone of the heroic type who thinks differently.

Of Agamemnon's greatness, there can be no doubt. The Homeric epithet most commonly associated with him is "lord of men"—the greatest ruler among the mortals. He is the leader of the expedition against Troy, the outcome of which, everyone understands, will decisively shape the world. At one particularly dark moment in the battle, Agamemnon broods on the consequences of defeat: "Our memory blotted out a world away from Argos!" (XIV 84–85). Oblivion: It's a terrible prospect for a fellow as accustomed to glory as Agamemnon.

But though Agamemnon is the greatest ruler, he is not the greatest warrior. That distinction belongs to Achilles, "best of the Achaeans." Both facts are known to both men, and to the Achaean and Trojan ranks alike. To understand how the inner greatness of a hero expresses itself, we have looked at the second phase of Achilles's rage in the *Iliad*, that over the death of Patroclus. To see just how great a threat such a hero can be to even the greatest king, we can look at the first phase of the rage of Achilles, his row with Agamemnon.

Like the Trojan War itself, which began with the Trojan prince Paris stealing the fabulously beautiful Helen away from the Spartan King Menelaeus, the quarrel between Achilles and Agamemnon also starts out over a woman. As the *Iliad* opens, the Achaeans have been besieging Troy for nine years. They are frustrated and tired, and what's more, a plague has now broken out in their ranks. The obvious conclusion is that the gods are angry. But why?

In addition to laying siege to Troy, Agamemnon's forces, often led by Achilles, have been sacking Troy's allies in the neighborhood. In the course of one such venture (before the action of the *Iliad* begins), Agamemnon has taken the beautiful Chryseis, daughter of a priest of the temple of Apollo, for his concubine as a battle prize.

So that explains to the satisfaction of pretty much everyone, except Agamemnon, who among the gods is punishing them—Apollo—and why. At a tense assembly of the leading Achaeans, Achilles warns that defeat at Troy is imminent unless Agamemnon does the right thing and gives Chryseis back.

The "lord of men" doesn't like this a bit. But he soon assents, with the proviso that if he must give up Chryseis, he will take another prize in her stead, lest he "alone of the Argives go without my honor." We note here that Agamemnon's sense of self, his own greatness, is (so to say) other-directed. It requires validation: glory and prizes. A world in which all the "men" of the "lord of men" get prizes and the lord himself does not get a prize is a world turned upside-down. The legitimacy of the king requires constant acknowledgment by those who owe him their allegiance.

Achilles tries to appeal to a sense of honor in Agamemnon higher than the demand for a trophy fit for a king. Achilles points out that all the booty has already been distributed among the fighters: "collect it, call it back from the rank and file? *That* would be the disgrace" (I 147–148). It would be conduct unbefitting the "lord of men." Achilles tries to direct Agamemnon's sense of honor inward. He also suggests that after Apollo has been appeased with the return of Chryseis, and the Achaeans defeat the Trojans, Agamemnon will have prizes aplenty.

Achilles's comments only escalate Agamemnon's sense of indignity. The king says that in the absence of other compensation for giving Chryseis back, he will take a different captive for his concubine—perhaps, come to think of it, Achilles's own Briseis.

Agamemnon's response infuriates Achilles, whose appeal to an inner sense of honor instantly vanishes. Instead, he gives voice directly to an exceedingly delicate albeit largely unspoken subject: the tension between the greatest king and the greatest warrior. Achilles essentially claims that he has been doing Agamemnon a favor by fighting on his side. He points out that he and his Myrmidons never had a quarrel of their own with

Priam. They came "to fight for you, to win your honor back from the Trojans" (I 187–188). Achilles feels that Agamemnon has now slighted him, disgraced him. He, Achilles, is the best warrior. His comment here indicates he may think Agamemnon on his own might not be up to the task of winning against the Trojans. Achilles is, moreover, a Myrmidon king, not an Argive subject of Agamemnon's. He *owes* Agamemnon no allegiance—except, perhaps, in the sense that he has previously agreed to join with Agamemnon in the war with Troy.

Yet in the view of the greatest warrior, the rewards in prizes and glory have not been at all commensurate with his deeds:

> "[ . . . ] My honors never equal yours,
> whenever we sack some wealthy Trojan stronghold—
> my arms bear the brunt of the raw, savage fighting,
> true, but when it comes to dividing up the plunder
> the lion's share is yours, and back I go to my ships,
> clutching some scrap, some pittance I love,
> when I have fought to exhaustion." (I 193–199)

Here, then, the relationship of the greatest warrior to the greatest king dissolves into a one-sided exercise in resentment. In the heat of the moment, Achilles loses touch with the inner sense of greatness that has been largely responsible for his heroic deeds, instead focusing on the insufficiency of the prizes he has won in compensation for them. He is right that the prizes have been inadequate to his achievements, but he is wrong, of course, in thinking that better prizes would have somehow satisfied him. Unlike Agamemnon, for whom the prizes are an essential acknowledgment of his authority as "lord of men," the greatest warrior in his heart knows he needs no such acknowledgment, that he alone is master and judge of himself. This becomes burningly clear once Patroclus dies, as we have seen in the previous chapter. Now, however, Achilles threatens to walk out on Agamemnon, to quit the war and go home to Phthia.

Achilles's complaint enrages Agamemnon further. With Achilles both denying the authority of Agamemnon over him and calling into question the fairness of his treatment at the hand of the lord of men, the confrontation between the two is getting into very dangerous territory. Agamemnon now chooses to belittle Achilles's martial prowess as something for which Achilles himself deserves no credit: It is "just a gift of god" (I 211). He then paints Achilles as a deserter. The king warns him:

> "[. . . ] I will be there in person at your tents
> to take Briseis in all her beauty, your own prize—
> so you can learn just how much greater I am than you
> and the next man up may shrink from matching words with me,
> from hoping to rival Agamemnon strength for strength." (I 217–221)

At this, Achilles considers drawing his sword on Agamemnon. Homer describes the timely arrival of the goddess Athena, whom only Achilles can see. She urges him on behalf of herself and the goddess Hera to restrain himself: "Obey us both" (I 251). The appeal sways Achilles. He sheaths his sword and rounds once again verbally on Agamemnon, calling him a drunk and a coward, and admonishing him that the day will come when the Achaeans beg Achilles to return to fight for them.

Agamemnon is in turn unrelenting, berating Achilles:

> . . . "this soldier wants to tower over the armies,
> he wants to rule over all, to lord it over all,
> give out orders to every man in sight." (I 336–338)

Achilles replies that he himself would be a coward if he were willing to submit to any order Agamemnon chose to give: "Never again, *I* trust, will Achilles yield to *you*" (I 347). He says contemptuously that he won't fight over Briseis, since the Achaeans, having been the ones who gave her to him in the first place, could have her back if they want. But he informs Agamemnon in the bloodiest of language that he will kill him if he attempts to take anything else "against my will" (I 353).

The two part ways. Agamemnon arranges for the return of Chryseis. Achilles, for his part, is now so enraged that he importunes the gods to come to the aid of his erstwhile enemy, the Trojans, in battle. The weeping Achilles tells his goddess-mother Thetis that he wants to see the Achaeans driven from their siege of Troy back to their ships, there to be trapped and killed:

> "So all can reap the benefits of their king—
> so even mighty Atrides [Agamemnon] can see how mad he was
> to disgrace Achilles, the best of the Achaeans." (I 488–490)

Thus is the stage set for the action of the first third of the *Iliad*: The beleaguered Agamemnon and the Achaeans suffer the full weight of a Trojan onslaught as Achilles sulks in his tent.

First, Agamemnon defies Apollo, courting disaster. Second, Agamemnon proposes a course of action that Achilles must oppose as disgraceful. Finally, Agamemnon proposes to disgrace none other than Achilles himself. The bond between Agamemnon and Achilles is broken, seemingly irreparably.

Agamemnon and Achilles have different ideas about what honor entails. Agamemnon, the lord of men, sees his due as the greatest prize. Under favorable circumstances, Achilles would perhaps not object. In peacetime, each could repair to his own kingdom, there to receive as king top honors in the sense Agamemnon means. Even during wartime, when the war is going well for the Achaeans—when they are sacking the cities of Trojan allies and hauling off booty in surpassing quantity—the difference between receiving Chryseis or Briseis as a concubine is maybe not worth an argument. Yet the circumstances at the beginning of the *Iliad* are anything but favorable: nine long years into the siege of Troy, and a plague sweeping through the Achaean ranks.

Moreover, it is only wartime that allows for the disclosure of the distinction that exists between the greatest king and the greatest warrior. It is abundantly clear from the exchange between Agamemnon and Achilles in Book I that Achilles's martial superiority has long been a sore subject for Agamemnon, and Agamemnon's kingly superiority a sore subject for Achilles. The greatest warrior and the greatest king are not united in one person. Once their row is well under way and tempers are flaring, Agamemnon voices what seems like a long-harbored suspicion: that Achilles would like to displace Agamemnon as "lord of men." Although Achilles overcomes his impulse to try to kill Agamemnon, which might achieve the unity of greatest king and greatest warrior in the person of Achilles, he nevertheless does nothing to dispel Agamemnon's suspicion of his loyalty. Achilles says that only a coward would obey Agamemnon unquestioningly, promises to kill anyone who tries to take anything from him against his will, quits the fight, and beseeches higher powers for Agamemnon's defeat.

As a matter of first impression, Homer's presentation of the row between Agamemnon and Achilles in Book I is highly unfavorable to Agamemnon. The "lord of men" looks frankly petty, and we know from the first line that the *Iliad* is Achilles's story, meaning it is not Agamemnon's. But we should not leave matters at first impression. Homer has provided a more nuanced account.

We must begin with the observation, to which I have gestured above, that in the course of their argument before the assembly, Agamemnon is in fact in the process of backtracking—conceding all of Achilles's points. Agamemnon is angry with the seer who told him about Apollo's anger and how to dispel it, but he gets the message: He will return Chryseis. And he quickly abandons the idea of demanding loot back from his fighters. Moreover, it is entirely unclear that he is actually intending to enforce his musings about taking for himself somebody else's concubine. "Enough. We'll deal with all this later, in due time" (I 165), Agamemnon says, just before he begins giving instructions for Chryseis's return. There is a distinct possibility that "later" means "forget it." At a minimum, the problem requires more kingly thought. Yet Achilles chooses to interpret Agamemnon's clearly off-the-cuff comments as a premeditated assault on his honor and stature, adopting Agamemnon's view of honor and stature as requiring prizes and glory.

What Agamemnon has that Achilles lacks, and what Agamemnon above all must keep, is legitimacy as "lord of men"—king of Argos and top king among the Achaeans. But Agamemnon has not become king by fighting his way to the top; he is the son of King Atreus and is thus rightful heir to the throne of Argos. He needs the people around him to respect his authority as a matter of course, lest seeds of rebellion sprout and the political order constructed around the king become unstable. Yet respecting Agamemnon's authority is precisely what Achilles has boxed himself into the position of being unable to do. Agamemnon does not need Briseis and may not even want Briseis— until and unless someone tells Agamemnon he *can't have* Briseis. At that moment, the issue is no longer who gets which concubine, but the authority of the "lord of men." Agamemnon must put down challenges to his authority, by force if necessary. And the routine maintenance of that authority is intimately bound to the proposition that the king in principle deserves the biggest prize. With the unique responsibilities of the crown come the greatest rewards. Moreover, it is ultimately the king who has final say on who gets which prize. Perhaps he would choose to honor an especially valiant warrior with a uniquely valuable prize that he might otherwise keep for himself. But the decision is the king's, not the warrior's.

When Agamemnon's men show up at Achilles's tent for Briseis, Achilles turns her over voluntarily, as he said he would. If he did not, we would perforce go on to read a very different book: It would be the story of a struggle to the death for supreme political power between Agamemnon and Achilles. Such a book, in Homer's hands, would no doubt have been interesting—but not as interesting as the *Iliad*. What makes the *Iliad* more interesting is that it is not a struggle for political power, which is of no apparent interest to Achilles. There is no indication Achilles is afraid of fighting Agamemnon. Achilles has asserted that he will fight anyone who tries to take something from him against his will. Agamemnon, for his part, has expressed his willingness to fight for Briseis if he must, as a warning to others about the danger of defying the "lord of men." But the two headstrong wills do not collide. Agamemnon's primary purpose is the defense of his kingly authority, and Achilles is not interested in challenging him on the point. He demonstrates as much by his willingness to yield Briseis.

Achilles's position in the row with Agamemnon is to reject Agamemnon's authority over *himself*. Achilles answers only to the gods. At the heart of the *Iliad* is the self-struggle of Achilles to assert his greatness— not to prove it to others, not to win the acclaim of others, not to rule over others, but to do his greatness justice by his own inner light. He is Agamemnon's biggest problem. And when you are the biggest problem of the "lord of men," you are a mighty big problem indeed.

In the end, the resolution of the conflict between the greatest warrior and the greatest king comes only with the foretold death, freely chosen, of the greatest warrior. Nevertheless, at the end of the penultimate book of the *Iliad*, Homer offers a subtle but poignant illustration of the relative stature of the two men. In tribute to Patroclus, Achilles has convened funeral games and put up lavish prizes for the fastest charioteer, best wrestler, best archer, and so forth. The last contest is throwing a spear, a task at which Agamemnon himself excels. As the lord of men is about to take on his challenger, Achilles calls it off:

> "Atrides [i.e., Agamemnon]—well we know how far you excel us all:
> no one can match your strength at throwing spears,
> You are the best by far!
> Take first prize [an ornate cauldron] and return to your hollow ships
> while we award this spear [the one that was to have been thrown in
>     the contest]

to the fighter Meriones,
if that would please your heart. That's what I propose."

And Agamemnon the lord of men could not resist. (XXIII, 986–992)

We recall the outbreak of the row between Agamemnon and Achilles, a dispute over a battle prize Agamemnon has bestowed upon himself, the concubine Chryseis. The row escalates into a challenge from Achilles to the very legitimacy and authority of Agamemnon as "lord of men." Its practical consequence is Achilles's withdrawal from battle and his prayer for the Achaeans' defeat, a prayer on the verge of being granted until the death of Patroclus brings Achilles decisively back into the fight.

Now Agamemnon gets a prize again, and a fine one it is indeed. Achilles also heaps lavish praise on Agamemnon, open acknowledgment of the primacy of "the lord of men." But this time it is not Agamemnon granting himself honors appropriate to his primacy, but Achilles who is doing the bestowing. Achilles repudiates his challenge to Agamemnon's authority, having realized that the accoutrements of greatness in the form of prizes and glory and even supreme political power are no measure of greatness within. The scene of the final encounter between the two in the *Iliad*, fewer than 20 lines in all, is almost chilling in its depiction of Achilles's self-assured, god-like superiority over the "lord of men," who cannot resist.

Although it is true that the majority of heroes from ancient times were men, the ability and at times the willingness to risk or give up one's life is not unique to men, nor is the danger such a willingness can pose to the established political order under the right circumstances. For one such female paragon, consider the (possibly legendary) case of Lucretia, a figure from the Rome of the sixth century BCE described by the later authors Dionysius of Halicarnassus and Titus Livy and the subject of a dramatic poem by Shakespeare.

Lucretia was the wife of Lucius Tarquinius Collatinus (anglicized as "Collatine"), a grand nephew of the king of Rome. Her husband was governor of Collatia, a town in Central Italy not far from Rome.

In Livy's version of the story, which became the basis of Shakespeare's retelling, Collatine was at a drinking party in Ardea with a number of royal princes, including Sextus Tarquinius (anglicized as Tarquin), son of the king and heir apparent. As the alcohol flowed, the men took to debating the question of whose wife was the most virtuous. Collatine declared that they could settle the matter at once by riding out at that very moment to see what their wives were up to. "What we see of the behaviour of each on the unexpected arrival of her husband, let that be the surest test," Collatine said (57). And so they did, riding first to Rome and then on to Collatia, where they discovered, first, all the king's daughters-in-law "passing their time in feasting and luxury" (57) and then Lucretia in Collatia late at night spinning her loom in the company of her handmaids. The princes all agreed that Lucretia deserved the palm in this competition.

But there was a dark side to the men's revelry. Tarquin became "inflamed by the beauty and exemplary purity of Lucretia" (57). In the Dionysius of H. version, there is no drinking party, but the king has dispatched Tarquin to Collatia on a military mission, and Lucretia has received him there with great hospitality (64). Whether, as in Livy, Tarquin traveled to Collatia for the purpose of having his way with Lucretia, or whether he conceived his plan on the spot, late the night of his arrival he stole into Lucretia's room. Brandishing a sword, Tarquin told Lucretia that she must submit willingly to him sexually, or he would kill her.

But even as Tarquin continued to entreat and threaten her, Lucretia would not submit. Livy says that Lucretia "was inflexible and not moved even by the fear of death" (58). So Tarquin escalated, seizing upon a threat to Lucretia that he sensed she would deem even worse than death: submit willingly to him sexually, or die and be dishonored. Tarquin told her that after he killed her, he would kill one of the household slaves, whose naked corpse he would position alongside her, claiming he found the two lovers *in flagrante delicto*.

The thought of this lasting dishonor, the desecration of her reputation for all time, was too much for Lucretia to bear. She chose to submit. In the Dionysius account, Tarquin accompanied his threat with a blandishment as well: If Lucretia willingly complied, he would marry her, and she would rule the Roman kingdom alongside him (65). But Dionysius portrays the offer of marriage as of no weight in Lucretia's decision to submit. Both paint portraits of a strong and virtuous woman who prided her virtue above all. When at last she gave in, it was to avoid the dishonor Tarquin had promised would accompany her death.

After Tarquin finally took his leave, Lucretia was beside herself with mortification. In Livy's account, she sent for her father to come from Rome and for her husband to come from Ardea, telling them each to bring a loyal friend along (58). In Dionysius's, which is rather more theatrical, Lucretia rode to her father's house in Rome, where she threw herself in tears at his feet and asked him to summon the leading figures of the city (66). The point is that Lucretia has chosen a public setting, with witnesses, for what will ensue.

The assembly completed, Lucretia unburdened herself of everything that had happened the previous night, and asked of those present that they avenge the wrong Tarquin did to her. Those assembled were shocked by the news, but what happened next was more shocking still. Immediately upon completion of her revelation, accusation, and demand for justice, she took out a dagger concealed in her dress and stabbed herself mortally in the heart.

As Dionysius describes what happened next: "This dreadful scene struck the Romans who were present with so much horror and compassion that they all cried out with one voice that they would rather die a thousand deaths in defence of their liberty than suffer such outrages to be committed by the tyrants" (67). In Livy's account, which has a little more going in the way of rhetorical flourish, Lucius Junius Brutus, whom Collatine brought with him from Ardea, withdrew the bloody knife from

Lucretia's breast and solemnly declared, "By this blood—most pure before the outrage wrought by the king's son—I swear, and you, O gods, I call to witness that I will drive hence Lucius Tarquinius Superbus, together with his cursed wife and his whole brood, with fire and sword and every means in my power, and I will not suffer them or any one else to reign in Rome" (59).

And that's what happened. Brutus took charge of the rebellion, marching to Rome. As Livy writes: "The terrible occurrence created no less excitement in Rome than it had done in Collatia; there was a rush from all quarters of the City to the Forum" (59). There, Brutus retold the story of the rape of Lucretia by the son of the king, and other abuses by the ruler of Rome. Livy: "By enumerating these and, I believe, other still more atrocious incidents which his keen sense of the present injustice suggested, but which it is not easy to give in detail, he goaded on the incensed multitude to strip the king of his sovereignty and pronounce a sentence of banishment against Tarquin with his wife and children" (59). The revolution ended with the royal family in exile, Tarquin himself soon to be murdered "in revenge for the old feuds he had kindled by his rapine and murders" (60), and Brutus and Collatine named the first consuls of the new Roman Republic.

Why did Lucretia take her life? Consider her own explanation. Her last words in Livy before stabbing herself are blood-chilling: "It is for you . . . to see that [Tarquin] gets his deserts; although I acquit myself of the sin, I do not free myself from the penalty; no unchaste woman shall henceforth live and plead Lucretia's example" (58). She cannot really prove that she is blameless, and therefore that she deserves to live, except by taking her own life. In the absence of the deed, she is just a teller of tales. In her case, the tale is true. But of others to come, who knows? She will not provide a model for those who would behave unchastely and tell tales to escape just punishment.

Taking her own life is the ultimate proof of her accusation against Tarquin. He is, after all, the son of the king and heir to the throne: the second most important Roman of all after his father. Had she merely accused him, he could have denied everything; at worst, he could have portrayed the sexual initiative as her own. There were, after all, no signs of physical abuse. He said/she said. It seems reasonably safe to say that the legal procedures of sixth century BCE Rome probably didn't favor a woman making an accusation against a powerful man. But for what conceivable reason would a woman who had *not* been treated as Lucretia said Tarquin treated her come forward entirely of her own volition, make such an accusation, *and then kill herself?*

But it is not, finally, a desire for revenge against Tarquin that motivates her: Rather, her motivation is to establish by deed her rectitude in her own light—even though the only deed sufficient to do so will cost her life.

Here is Shakespeare giving voice to Lucretia as she is pondering what to do:

> "O, that is gone for which I sought to live,
> And therefore now I need not fear to die. (151)
> * * *
>
> For me, I am the mistress of my fate,
> And with my trespass never will dispense,
> Till life to death acquit my forced offence." (153)

Here, honor is all: but honor is not "honors" bestowed by others. As in the case of Achilles in his rage over Patroclus, it is inner greatness expressing itself. Lucretia's honor is a god-like perfection beyond the capacity of death to erase—and indeed, may require her death, as it does here, to express itself fully. Here's more of Shakespeare's presentation of her interior monologue:

> "My honour I'll bequeath unto the knife
> That wounds my body so dishonoured.
> 'Tis honour to deprive dishonour'd life;
> The one will live, the other being dead:

So of shame's ashes shall my fame be bred;
For in my death I murder shameful scorn:
My shame so dead, mine honour is newborn." (170)

Lucretia's suicide is a deed for the ages because of the perfection of honor her fearlessness achieves. Oh yes, and it brought to an end the 25-year reign of Lucius Tarquinius Superbus and the 224-year-old kingdom of Rome. The heroic type, facing death without fear in fulfillment of a sense of inner greatness, can indeed be a menace to society.

The fall of the kingdom of Rome was not something Lucretia appeared to have sought, but rather a consequence of a chain of events she set in motion. It seems likely that she would not have been displeased by the news of the exiled Tarquin's murder, nor of the demise of a dynasty whose corruption her rape made plain. But it seems equally unlikely that she would have felt in any way triumphant. Such an emotion would have been entirely extraneous to her purpose and resolve. She achieved perfect justice to herself and her honor in her final act, her suicide. Nothing was missing. When she said, "It is for you to see that he gets his deserts," her point was not to demand that her witnesses seek justice for her sake, but rather to suggest that they do so for their own—because all those hearing her story and witnessing her emphatic demonstration of its truth ought properly to be compelled for reasons of their own honor to act against Tarquin. That her witnesses rose to the occasion speaks well of them. The historic consequences of their willingness to take up arms to see that Tarquin gets his deserts commend her heroism to us. But they add nothing to the perfection of her honor, which she achieved solely on her own account.

I suppose it would be possible to take the side of the Roman dynasty in its dispute with the avengers of Lucretia, perhaps on the grounds that although Tarquin was reprehensible and deserved his ignominy and death, his crime did not warrant overthrowing the king. But I know of no one who has made that case, in literary or other terms. Lucretia is purely heroic, first in her willingness to give up her own life out of obligation to her inner perfection, second in the universal post facto acclaim of others for her action and for the outcome of the ensuing chain of events.

The latter element, the acclaim after the fact, is by no means a certain by-product of the heroic willingness to risk death. Others who have put their lives on the line out of a sense of inner greatness, and who have posed a mortal threat to existing political order, have been more ambiguous figures in terms of the conclusions people have reached about the rectitude of their actions.

Coriolanus, a possibly mythical figure, was a great warrior who won glorious victories for Rome in the first years of the Republic. Plutarch describes his character from his first foray into battle, where he won a laurel for saving the life of another Roman soldier:

> It would seem that when a young man's ambition is no integral part of his nature, it is apt to be quenched by an honourable distinction which is attained too early in life; his thirst and fastidious appetite are speedily satisfied. But serious and firm spirits are stimulated by the honours they receive, and glow brightly, as if roused by a mighty wind to achieve the manifest good. They do not feel that they are receiving a reward for what they have done, but rather that they are giving pledges of what they will do, and they are ashamed to fall behind their reputation instead of surpassing it by their actual exploits. It was in this spirit that Marcius [dubbed "Coriolanus" after his victory over the Volsci at Corioli] vied with himself in manly valour, and being ever desirous of fresh achievement, he followed one exploit with another, and heaped spoils upon spoils, so that his later commanders were always striving with their predecessors in their efforts to do him honour, and to surpass in their testimonials to his prowess. (IV)

Pressed to seek political office, as was the custom for successful generals, Coriolanus expected no less from the people of Rome than that they spontaneously acknowledge his worthiness to lead them. He was reluctant to pander to them in order to obtain their approval—to show them the scars from the wounds he suffered fighting for Rome, per custom. In Shakespeare's version, Coriolanus is consulting with his counselor Menenius Agrippa and two tribunes of the people, Junius Brutus and Sicinius Velutus, who are hostile to his aristocratic bearing:

**MENENIUS**
The senate, Coriolanus, are well pleased
To make thee consul.
**CORIOLANUS**
I do owe them still
My life and services.
**MENENIUS**
It then remains
That you do speak to the people.
**CORIOLANUS**
I do beseech you,
Let me o'erleap that custom, for I cannot
Put on the gown, stand naked and entreat them,
For my wounds' sake, to give their suffrage: please you
That I may pass this doing.
**SICINIUS**
Sir, the people
Must have their voices; neither will they bate
One jot of ceremony.
**MENENIUS**
Put them not to't:
Pray you, go fit you to the custom and
Take to you, as your predecessors have,
Your honour with your form.
**CORIOLANUS**
It is a part
That I shall blush in acting, and might well
Be taken from the people.

**BRUTUS**

Mark you that?

**CORIOLANUS**

To brag unto them, thus I did, and thus;

Show them the unaching scars which I should hide,

As if I had received them for the hire

Of their breath only! (Act II, scene 2, 134–155)

Coriolanus finally decided to go through with the required ritual of baring his wounds in the Forum and asking the people for their support. But he seems to have hated himself for doing so, musing halfway through the ordeal:

> Better it is to die, better to starve,
>
> Than crave the hire which first we do deserve.
>
> To beg of Hob and Dick, that do appear,
>
> Their needless vouches? Custom calls me to't:
>
> What custom wills, in all things should we do't,
>
> The dust on antique time would lie unswept,
>
> And mountainous error be too highly heapt
>
> For truth to o'er-peer. Rather than fool it so,
>
> Let the high office and the honour go
>
> To one that would do thus. I am half through;
>
> The one part suffer'd, the other will I do. (Act II, scene 3, 121–132)

He did indeed win the support of the people, and he withdrew from the Forum in expectation of his consulship. But the conniving tribunes, in Shakespeare's telling, saw an opportunity to step forward and turn the people against Coriolanus by revealing his contempt for them. When the people subsequently switched sides and spurned Coriolanus as arrogant, he denounced popular rule as mere appeal to a rabble. His political enemies had him banished from Rome.

Whereupon Coriolanus himself switched sides. He joined his old battlefield enemy, Tullus Aufidius, the king of the Volsci, and led the Volscian army into battle against Rome, the unworthy city of his birth. Only the intervention of his mother at the eleventh hour, with the Volscian army on the verge of overrunning Rome, dissuaded Coriolanus from destroying the city he might have led as consul, had he only been willing to do what he was manifestly incapable of doing: appealing for the support of those he regarded as unworthy to judge him. Coriolanus instead brokered a peace between Rome and the Volsci. But the deal infuriated Aufidius, who was reveling in the prospect of his imminent conquest (though he was at best ambivalent about his reliance on Coriolanus for the chance). In the end, the bitter Aufidius induced a mob to set upon Coriolanus and kill him.

Plutarch remarks that "whereas other men found in glory the chief end of valour, he found the chief end of glory in his mother's gladness": Coriolanus saved Rome for mom's sake. In Shakespeare's telling, as Coriolanus saw his mother, wife, and son approaching camp, he reflects

My wife comes foremost; then the honour'd mould
Wherein this trunk was framed [Coriolanus's mother], and in her hand
The grandchild to her blood. But, out, affection!
All bond and privilege of nature, break!
Let it be virtuous to be obstinate.
What is that curt'sy worth? or those doves' eyes,
Which can make gods forsworn? I melt, and am not
Of stronger earth than others. My mother bows;
As if Olympus to a molehill should
In supplication nod: and my young boy
Hath an aspect of intercession, which
Great nature cries 'Deny not.' Let the Volsces
Plough Rome and harrow Italy: I'll never
Be such a gosling to obey instinct, but stand,

As if a man were author of himself
And knew no other kin. (Act V, scene 3, 22–38)

Coriolanus's resolve to "be obstinate" in the face of his family's entreaties did not hold up, nor was he able to "stand" as "author of himself," his heroic effort to do so notwithstanding. Perhaps there is a type of being that stands as "author of" itself, but a human who seeks to do so is a self-contradiction, desiring to be something a human *is not*. Had Coriolanus been able to withstand the entreaties of his family, had he proceeded to destroy Rome and his family along with it, he would still not have been "author of himself" insofar as he sought to make of himself something a human cannot be.

The heroism of Achilles and Lucretia is not tragic. Their willingness to face death is not a rebellion against their humanity but an embrace of it. They are each "great in their greatness" and completely human at one and the same time. Coriolanus *is* a tragic hero. He wanted to be something no human can be. The death he encountered as a result was no affirmation of his heroic heart or sense of his own greatness, but rather a rebuke to a sense of greatness seeking to extend itself beyond the human. Death has a way of reminding one of one's humanity in the event one has forgotten it, and it was coming for Coriolanus whether or not he destroyed Rome. But for Rome, destruction or survival was a pretty close call. Deluded or undeluded, the heroic type can pose grave danger.

Alcibiades burst on the scene of fifth century BCE Athens like a supernova. He was a beautiful, brilliant, well-born young man, rumored to have been the lover of his teacher Socrates. Alcibiades figures prominently in two dialogues of Plato, one of which bears his name, both of which ostensibly treat the subject of love but also address his spectacular political ambition and the attempt of Socrates to place some checks on it for Alcibiades's own good.

This Socrates sought to do by transforming the traditional erotic desire of an older Athenian man for a boy into the desire of the boy for the older man. The reversed attraction would then make the boy receptive to the advice of the older man—in the case of Alcibiades, to come to a better understanding of the world and himself before throwing himself headlong into politics.

In Plato's telling, Socrates turned the erotic trick neatly. In the *Symposium*, Plato depicts an older Alcibiades turning up drunk at a dinner and drinking party where Socrates and others have devoted themselves to praise of Eros, or erotic love. Alcibiades delivers an impassioned speech in which he rebukes Socrates for never having made love to him.

Yet the second element of Socrates's project, the taming of the ambition of Alcibiades, we must judge a rather comprehensive failure. Alcibiades came to fame during the Peloponnesian War for advocating bold attacks on Sparta. Unfortunately, the expedition to Sicily that he proposed Athens undertake ended in disaster. Thereafter, Alcibiades fell into political disfavor.

No longer in possession of a position of political prominence in the city of his birth, Alcibiades, like Coriolanus, simply switched sides. He went to war against Athens on the side of Sparta and won several important victories for his former enemies. But possibly as a result of an affair with the wife of Agis, the Spartan king, Alcibiades soon found himself unwelcome in Sparta—at which point he defected yet again, this time to the Persian satrap Tissaphernes. Alcibiades encouraged Persia to allow the Athenians and the Spartans to wear themselves down in war, then to invade Attica and drive the Greeks out; all the while, however, he was conniving successfully with a faction in Athens to get himself recalled from exile and installed as military commander. He was assassinated, probably on the orders of the victorious Spartan general Lysander, in 404, but not before demonstrating that Athens, Sparta, and the Persian Empire combined were too small to contain his ambition. One must give credit to Socrates for his insight into the problematic nature of the character of Alcibiades, even if Socrates was unable to do anything about it.

Was there a real Achilles? If not exactly the hero Homer depicts, perhaps one whose exploits in a long-ago war lived on and were further embellished in stories passed orally from generation to generation before Homer codified them in the *Iliad*? No one knows. Likewise Lucretia and Coriolanus. Of course insofar as the latter two served as subject matter for Shakespeare and are much better known to us through his renderings than through the sources on which he relied, one must acknowledge the possibility that Shakespeare's accounts reflect the disposition and prejudices of the fifteenth century more than they do authentic insight into the heroism of the characters he depicts.

But having acknowledged the possibility, I now propose to dismiss it as irrelevant to the purpose of this exercise, which is an exploration of heroism in the ancient and modern world and the ways in which the heroic type shapes politics and the political world shapes heroism. Homer has achieved a near-perfect rendition of the highest heroic type of his age, a single character who brings into focus both the inner-directed greatness of that type and the mortal peril such greatness poses to the legitimacy and authority of political order. The achievement of Shakespeare is on a comparable scale. Homer's and Shakespeare's characters are literary gifts for the ages, and Plato's dialogues, meanwhile, offer a profound account of the difficult problem posed by the heroic ambition of an Alcibiades. If these characters are in some sense idealized, so be it; the real-world political issues they pose remain.

The ancient world offers no better illustration of this than the far better-documented case of a certain Gaius Julius Caesar. He was, quite simply, the most ambitious Roman of all among a polity in which ambition on a grand scale was a familiar sight. Here's Plutarch:

> Caesar's many successes . . . did not divert his natural spirit of enterprise and ambition to the enjoyment of what he had laboriously achieved, but served as fuel and incentive for future achievements, and begat in him plans for greater deeds and a passion for fresh glory, as though he had used up what he already had. What he felt was therefore nothing else than emulation of himself, as if he had been another man, and a sort of rivalry between what he had done and what he purposed to do. (58)

Plutarch is sometimes accused of reading too much ambition into Julius Caesar from too early on, as if Caesar had always had designs on installing himself as the sole and exclusive ruler of Rome and its vast territorial holdings (some of which he conquered or subdued personally, most notably Gaul and Spain). Perhaps there is justice to this charge. On the other hand, one is hard-pressed to find a moment of decision in the record of Caesar's life in which he did anything but press his ambition more fully, from standing for the office of pontifex maximus, or chief priest, against two far more senior and more distinguished men than he (Caesar won, of course) down to the lavish dinner parties he threw for friends and rivals and the spectacles he produced for the people's enjoyment.

For example, Roman generals, upon their return home from an especially successful campaign, were eligible for the Senate to grant them a triumph—a spectacular military parade into the city in which the conqueror, resplendent in a laurel crown and a gold-embroidered toga on a four-horse chariot, would march his (disarmed) army and display his captive enemies in chains, often en route to their execution, along with their captured weapons, their treasures, exotic animals from their lands, and whatever else might impress, all to the cheers of the Roman multitude. There was no greater glory for a conquering hero.

When Caesar got back from subduing Spain, however, he faced a dilemma. He was surely deserving of a triumph. But to enjoy it, he would have to wait outside Rome, per law and custom, until the Senate approved it. Meanwhile, however, elections for consul were imminent, and Caesar wanted to stand for Rome's highest office. Doing so required him to be in the city. Without hesitation, he decided to forgo his triumph. He entered the city quietly, won the consulship, and never looked back. It's a sequence of events that goes a long way toward vindicating Plutarch's judgment that Caesar was someone whose "successes . . . begat in him plans for greater deeds and a passion for fresh glory."

Caesar was also a wit. One sometimes hears praise of the "self-deprecating wit" of prominent individuals—Henry Kissinger, for example: "The nice thing about being a celebrity is that, if you bore people, they think it's their fault." The self-deprecation is willful, of course, in that most practitioners of witticism of this sort, Kissinger not excepted, have a very large sense of self to deprecate. The wit of Julius Caesar shares such a sense of self, but spares us the bogus deprecation. It's the charm of a man who knows who he is and where he stands in relation to others, which is to say, above them. Upon passing through a small, dirt-poor, godforsaken barbarian village in the Alps on the way from Spain, he remarked to companions, "I would rather be first here than second at Rome." He was said to be found weeping one day while reading a history of Greece at the time of Alexander, and when friends asked why he was so sad, he replied, "Do you not think . . . it is matter for sorrow that while Alexander, at my age, was already king of so many peoples, I have as yet achieved no brilliant success?" The translation is stilted, but the humor lies in the irony, and the irony is that Caesar is serious. Most famous of all is "Veni, vidi, vici," the totality of a letter he wrote to a friend in Rome after his victory at Tila securing Lower Armenia from rebellion. It takes a certain sense of self to put matters in those terms. Caesar was writing a man called Amantius, but surely he knew he was also issuing a quip for the ages.

As Caesar was about to cross the Rubicon river with his army in 49 BCE, thus plunging Rome into a civil war from which he would emerge as first in Rome, the Republic never to recover, he is said to have become introspective: "To refrain from crossing will bring me misfortune; but to cross will bring misfortune to all men." There is, of course, considerable dispute over the accuracy of the quotation. In this version, it has an elegiac quality that is a little at odds with the verve of most of Caesar's aperçus. It might have been more in keeping with the man if he actually put it this way: *If I cross, I bring misfortune on everyone. If I don't, I bring it on myself.* His next words: "The die is cast." In the end, for a person of Caesar's classically heroic makeup, it's not an especially difficult question whether to plunge all of the Roman Republic into chaos and civil war or to endure the frustration of his own ambition. Others are expendable, a means to the end of the pursuit of worldly manifestations of a matchless inner-driven sense of greatness.

Caesar had a close call in the course of the civil war that brought him to power: at one point, Pompey the Great, representing the forces of the Republic against Caesar's bid for supreme power, had the drop on Caesar and his army. But rather than advance and deliver a crushing blow, Pompey withdrew out of a sense of caution. In Plutarch's account, Caesar's reaction on narrowly escaping was this: "Today victory had been with the enemy, if they had had a victor in command." So much for Pompey "the Great." To drip contempt for a man who could have wiped you out for his failure to do so: Again, this is a view from a high place.

In Shakespeare's *Julius Caesar*, Caesar dies at the beginning of the third act, most of the play still to come. The play is a tragedy, but it is not the tragedy of Caesar. The tragedy is that of Marcus Brutus, who joined the conspiracy to kill Caesar out of the belief that Caesar's ambition would destroy Rome. It turned out that Caesar's ambition had already destroyed Rome. Brutus was right, but the time had passed for any possibility of remedial action to restore the Republic. The play bears Caesar's name because of the magnitude of what Caesar wrought.

Caesar was assassinated, but that does not make him a tragic figure. That would only be true if you think death is always a bad outcome. This is not the classical hero's perspective. Caesar, in living history, achieved exactly what he sought, risking his life all along the way. Five hundred years of the Roman Republic, at the time the greatest political achievement human beings had wrought? Caesar destroyed that, one of the most astounding acts of destruction in the history of politics. That's how dangerous he was. On the other hand, and this is the subject of our next chapter, he was also a classical hero capable of founding an empire.

## CHAPTER 3

# THE HERO-KING

*The hero as founder, ruler, conqueror.*

The heroic type is willing to risk and even accept death as a consequence of action in accordance with an inner sense of greatness or exceptional virtue. As we have seen, this willingness can have far-ranging consequences for the political order into which a hero is born. The Achaeans came within a whisker of being driven from Troy while Achilles, their best warrior, sulked in his tent. The spectacular suicide of Lucretia, a woman wronged, brought down the dynasty that ruled Rome. Alcibiades of Athens and Coriolanus of Rome, once leading political figures, harbored ambitions so large in scale that when their homelands seemed to be seeking to constrain them, they were prepared to switch sides and make war on their own people. Julius Caesar, notwithstanding his conquests and honors, was not content to be anything less than the greatest man in Rome, and if that meant a civil war and the destruction of the Republic, so be it.

I have begun with examples of the danger the heroic type poses to political order. The reasons for doing so are several. The first is that the appearance on the political scene of a classically heroic character is a problem relatively remote from the modern world. Our practice of politics no longer has a typically life-or-death character, and so sometimes we need to remind ourselves of what politics was like when it did.

In addition, the politics of the ancient world turned on the decisions of powerful individuals in a way that is somewhat alien to our experience. There are no contemporary figures styled "lord of men." This has something to do with the broader-based political participation characteristic of the modern world versus the typical rule by king or tyrant in the ancient world, and we will get to that. But it also has something to do with the character of power as such.

In the ancient world, power begins in the body and in the character of the powerful human being, manifesting itself outwardly beginning with raw physical prowess. Achilles—he himself—led his Myrmidons into battle, where combat was of the most intimate sort. Poor Tros lived long enough to beg for mercy personally from the greatest warrior, and probably long enough after that for his last living perception to be the realization Achilles was denying his request. In the ancient world, a commander exercising power began with physical violence personally unleashed on the enemy and extended it from there thanks to an ability to motivate his army to strike out similarly. And, of course, a hero did as a hero wished. Anyone who might wish to thwart a hero's will needed to be prepared for a fight to the death.

To be sure, the president of the United States is a very powerful person, arguably the most powerful in the world, commander-in-chief of a huge war-making capacity including the ability to unleash a nuclear apocalypse. But the type of power a president wields is very different from that which Achilles and Caesar possessed. The power of the American president is institutional rather than personal, let alone physical. The president commands in wartime by speaking, by giving orders to senior officers who in turn give orders down the chain of command to the point at which violence begins (and usually ends). Moreover, the latitude for action of the constitutional commander-in-chief is hardly without limit. Military officers are required to obey lawful orders, but they are not required to obey unlawful orders. Refusing to obey an order might well result in a short-term crisis. But then again, in the highly unlikely event that an American president ordered a nuclear attack against a country in the absence of provocation of any kind, it seems still more unlikely, indeed vanishingly unlikely, that the military would carry out such an order.

There are a few notable exceptions, including Lucretia, but by and large the art of which the heroes of the ancient world were masters was that of personally slaying their enemies. George H.W. Bush, as commander in chief of the United States military at the time, led a multinational coalition of military forces that ejected Saddam Hussein from Kuwait in 1991, nullifying Saddam's attempt to claim Kuwait as a province of Iraq. Many Iraqi soldiers died in the course of the operation. Yet Bush as commander is rarely described in terms of the death he personally dealt to Iraq's military. Achilles on the rampage literally had blood on his hands, as a result of the intimate process of slaying one's enemies in his day. If Bush had "blood on his hands," the phrase was a figure of speech evoking that distant era but also on reflection reminding us how far we are from it.

So the political order of the ancient world was highly subject to disruption by powerful figures willing to risk death—in other words, the heroic type. We need to confront this bloody and dangerous pattern, so at odds with political order and change in our world, on its own terms.

Yet the ancient world was not merely anarchic. Perhaps there was a time when Hobbes's notional state of nature and "the war of every man against every man" was literally true, but it certainly does not describe the world of the Trojan War. By then, the political world had discernible political entities, including independent city-states and large-scale empires, some of them centuries old. The Greek gods, in the Greek imagination, were a rather capricious bunch, but the Greeks did not regularly switch out their gods for a new and improved set. Hobbes is certainly correct, however, that stable political order is not the natural condition of human beings. It has to come from somewhere.

Or rather, from some*one*. On one hand, the ancient world was subject to disruption and upheaval at the behest of the heroic type. But on the other hand, the political order of that ancient world was also largely *shaped* by the heroic type, powerful figures willing to risk death to impose their will. Rather than the hero-disruptor, we have the conquering hero or the hero as founder and lawgiver of a new state. Here, the hero's task is to begin the institutionalization of raw, heroic power—to move from its embodiment in the hero's personal physical and mental prowess to its investiture in the structures, organs, and procedures of a state and a government. Here, a heroic individual makes use of heroic power to constitute a political order of a kind the hero deems most desirable.

*The oldest solution to the problem of the hero in politics was, in effect, a merger: the hero as king.* The greatest would rule. Minos, the ancient king of Crete, was said by Socrates to have possessed a unique insight into how to rule. The laws he laid down, which became the basis for the laws of powerful Sparta, had been the longest continuously in force throughout the Greek world, making them (according to Socrates, anyway) worthy of respect and veneration. Minos was the strongest as well as the ruler. He founded the first city-state, and thus political order as Socrates knew it and we still know it. Minos was a synthesis of hero and king.

Machiavelli's *The Prince*, probably the most famous book about politics ever written, is at one level a philosophical exploration of the role of fortune and nature in human affairs, but at a more basic level a handbook on how to retain supreme political power. A successful prince is one who is able to throw off the yoke of moral stricture, wherever it may come from, and act solely in accordance with self-interest: "For a man who wants to make a profession of good in all regards must come to ruin among so many who are not good. Hence it is necessary to a prince, if he wants to maintain himself, to learn to be able not to be good, and to use this and not use it according to necessity" (XV).

There are advantages to a prince *appearing* to be moral and upright, but a prince unwilling to do evil when necessary will quickly be undone. The occupation of prince is inherently dangerous, insofar as there are always ambitious figures who would like to take one's place: "a prince should have two fears: one within, on account of his subjects; the other outside, on account of external powers" (XIX). The successful prince is one who remakes himself in accordance with these legitimate fears.

Machiavelli has no use for the idea of heroism in *The Prince*, but his counsel amounts to a short course in the brutally heroic. He writes:

> A prince should have no other object, or any other thought, nor take anything else as his art but that of war and its orders and disciplines; for that is the only art of concern to one who commands. And it is of such virtue that not only does it maintain those who have been born princes but many times it enables men of private fortune to rise to that rank; and on the contrary one sees that when princes have thought more of amenities than arms, they have lost their states. (XIV)

Machiavelli is adamant to the point of radicalism on the primacy of the commander's art:

> The principal foundations that all states have, new ones as well as old or mixed, are good laws and good arms. And because there cannot be good laws where there are not good arms, and where there are good arms there must be good laws, I shall leave out the reasoning on laws and shall speak of arms. (XII)

Machiavelli's peacetime counsel is vigilant preparation for war, physical and mental. On the physical side, when a prince isn't at war his first responsibility is to maintain his "good arms," and he should also engage in vigorous outdoor activity, conditioning himself for the hardship of battle. "[A]s to the exercise of the mind," he continues,

> a prince should read histories and consider in them the actions of excellent men, should see how they conducted themselves in wars, should examine the causes of their victories and losses, so as to be able to avoid the latter and imitate the former. Above all he should do as some excellent man has done in the past who found someone to imitate

who had been praised and glorified before him, whose exploits and actions he always kept beside himself, as they say Alexander the Great imitated Achilles; Caesar, Alexander; Scipio, Cyrus. (XIV)

Machiavelli recommends imitation of the winning ways of "excellent men," by which he means neither more nor less than successful princes and commanders. The extent to which such men exemplified classical virtues in the manner of an Aristotelean gentleman or Christian virtue as limned by Saint Paul is of no matter to Machiavelli—or rather, evidence of the possession of such traits is almost in itself a cause for suspicion about whether the prince in question had the ability "not to be good" when necessary. Figures worthy of princely emulation are cut from the classically heroic cloth we have been examining. Yet the imitation is not the same as the original. Risking one's life is inevitable for a ruler or for one who wants to be a ruler and is not especially noteworthy, and Machiavelli substitutes self-interest or self-aggrandizement for the inner sense of one's greatness we have found in classical heroism in its purest form. Another way to look at it is that Machiavelli *reduces* the sense of inner greatness to self-interest and ambition. His sense of "virtue" seems at times to be nothing other than what is useful to attain power and maintain oneself in it.

Thus, Machiavelli is engaged in *The Prince* in teaching rulers how to keep their crowns by remaking themselves, as necessary, in a quasi-heroic mold. They must be more dangerous than all comers, foreign or domestic. The priests will tell them what they *should* do, and Machiavelli rates the *appearance* of piety as a top trait of a successful prince. Indeed, it's probably fair to say that the best way to appear religious is actually to *be* religious. The same with appearing "merciful, faithful, humane, [and] honest" (XVII), other attributes Machiavelli identifies as useful for a prince to project for the purpose of maintaining himself in power. But that's provided, of course, that one knows when *not* to practice those very traits. The primary purpose of *The Prince* in its capacity as a practical guide is therefore to teach rulers when and how "not to be good."

Machiavelli, ever the controversialist, singles out for special praise Hiero of Syracuse, the brutal tyrant we met in the last chapter complaining ironically about how miserable the life of the tyrant is. Machiavelli praises him precisely *for* his brutality, the resoluteness with which he rose from nothing to seize absolute power and the shrewdness and the tenacity that allowed him to keep hold of it:

> From private individual he became prince of Syracuse, nor did he receive anything more from fortune than the opportunity. . . . Hiero eliminated the old military and started a new one; he left his old friendships and made new ones; and when he had friendships and soldiers of his own, he could build anything on top of such a foundation; . . . (VI)

Later, Machiavelli elaborates on Hiero's methods:

> When he, as I said, was made head of the army by the Syracusans, he knew immediately that their mercenary military was not useful. . . . Since he thought he could neither keep them nor let them go, he had them all cut to pieces, and then made war with his arms, not alien arms. (XIII)

The origins of Timur (or Tamerlane or Tamburlaine) the Great, the fourteenth-century conqueror of central and western Asia, were by most accounts likewise rather humble. His military prowess, however, was outsized, and with it he created an empire for himself in west, south, and central Asia, modeling his achievement on that of Genghis Khan and his Mongol Empire in the thirteenth century. Although the Mongol Empire continued to expand after Genghis Khan's death, the problem of dynastic succession was acute, as it would also become for Timur. Each ruler sought to divide control of the territory among sons who quickly set to warring among themselves. The resulting struggle for power was as much life-or-death as the conquest that preceded it. And while one must not shrink from the conclusion that Timur, like Genghis Khan before him, was superior in heroic qualities to his offspring, the latter were in general not remiss in the classically heroic quality we have been considering. The quiet life was not for the sons of Timur and Genghis Khan: they, like Dad, risked their lives in pursuit of their ambition.

Sometimes it worked out, sometimes not. Tokhtaymish, a descendant of Genghis Khan, was khan of the Blue Horde, one of the rivalrous pieces of the Golden Horde. Tokhtaymish seems to have been pretty good at the job, eventually reuniting (albeit briefly) the Golden Horde khanate under his rule. Unfortunately for him, he was deposed from that position in 1399 by the forces of none other than Timur, making Tokhtaymish one of history's losers.

Babur, a descendant of Timur, on the other hand, definitely made good on the bloodline. His autobiography, the *Baburnama*, believed to be the first such in Islamic literature, tells the story of the difficulties and dangers he encountered en route to establishing the Moghul Empire in India in the first decades of the sixteenth century. The matter-of-factness of the prose of the *Baburnama* misleadingly gives the impression that conquering a subcontinent is a fairly routine business, one step flowing from the previous. You can almost imagine yourself in Babur's place—which is all wrong. Babur was singularly heroic in achieving something many dreamed of but only he pulled off. Other authors might well sing his praise and point out the magnitude of what he did, as I am to a degree here. Embellishment, self-dramatization, even a congratulatory approach to his achievements doesn't occur to Babur because he is simply explaining what followed from his interior sense of his capabilities and ambition. That's enough.

It's no small thing to conquer west, south, and central Asia, or even most of one of them. Babur took his place as a state-founding hero alongside Romulus of Rome and Theseus of Athens (slayer, according to the legend, of King Minos's ferocious minotaur in the Labyrinth below Crete). Julius Caesar founded the Roman Empire. It does not go too far to say that until recently, all states have had a hero-founder at their inception. Rare as the type has been, the hero-founder's place was at the very origin of political order itself. The lasting historical influence of the emergence of a hero has often been not only the story of the heroism but also the history of the state the hero founded.

Machiavelli held that the "most excellent" of those who became princes "by their own virtue and not by fortune" were "Moses, Cyrus, Romulus, Theseus and the like" (VI). Leaving aside the question of who is "like" these four, he mentions the founders of Rome, Athens, the Persian Empire, and the Jewish people. The act of starting a polity, or a religion, essentially from scratch on the basis of an inner sense of how it should be ordered differently from other, existing polities or religions—and doing so in a fashion that outlasts the life of the founder by many generations, indeed millennia in the case of Moses—is, to Machiavelli, the highest form of political achievement (or at least the handiwork only of the "most excellent" practitioners of politics).

We all live in states founded by *someone*, whether in historical fact, like the United States of George Washington and the authors of the 1789 Constitution, or in a mythical tradition coming out of pre-historical tales, as with Romulus and Teresias. Simon Bolivar, the early nineteenth-century Venezuelan military leader, enjoys a reputation for greatness that spans Latin America for his role in liberating from Spanish rule not only Venezuela but also Peru, Ecuador, Panama, Colombia, and Bolivia, the country named after him. The World War I general Kamal Ataturk created the modern Turkish state out of the rubble of the dismembered Ottoman Empire. These founders continue to hold heroic status for their people.

They may have been in it for themselves, thinking not of others but of their own ambition to do great deeds. But when subsequent generations have thought of them, the descendants often attribute many of the benefits they enjoy to the great deeds of a hero-founder. They have sensed that their freedom, or city, nation, tribe, motherland, fatherland—the place they call home—had its origins in a hero who was acting on their behalf, whether that was the hero's intention or not.

Even that modern would-be world conqueror, Napoleon, got credit for more than simply military genius and outsized ambition: He brought the enlightenment of the "rights of man" and the Napoleonic Code with him on horseback. The philosopher G.W.F. Hegel detected the end of History and the arrival of the age of universal freedom and equality as he watched Napoleon prevail over the old-guard Prussian army at the battle of Jena in 1806. Napoleon served not just his own ambition and inner greatness, but all of humankind.

Was Moses a real, historical person? I think the contention of Machiavelli would be that "he" was, so long as by "he" we mean a figure capable of binding together a people under a new dispensation said to have divine origins. Machiavelli's point is that major religions and new political orders don't generate spontaneously; they are *begun*, founded by a founder, and such characters have historically exemplified and indeed must exemplify something of the classically heroic quality we have been describing.

I take no position on whether a certain Moses engaged in conversations with God. I note that scholars have long speculated that the mythologies and folklore traditions associated with various peoples have their roots in distant tales of actual hero-kings. Both Minos and Achilles were said to be sons of gods; their lineage was said to give them special powers or insight—to make them heroic. Maybe it's the other way around: Powers sometimes attributed to gods were an exaggeration of the power of actual human beings, whose heroics resonate from the recesses of pre-history as tales of the actions of gods. Some scholars believe that Väinämöinen, the Finnish god claimed to be central to the birth of the world, may have been an actual shaman or hero from the ninth century whose exploits were inflated in the retelling into godhood. Certainly a similar evolution could have taken place in the case of a man, Moses, some version of whom must have existed in order for the Hebrews to have been founded as a people, and his inspiration in the act of founding.

So we see that the problem of the hero in politics sometimes finds at least temporary resolution when heroes turn into kings. Likewise, some kings (though not all) turn out to be heroes.

Even those born heir to a throne have been at risk of the appearance on the scene of a heroic character who would not abide the existing political order. Some kings got lucky: No heroic types turned up on their watch, and they ruled uneventfully. But the only sure way for a king to achieve immunity from the political problem of collision with a hero was by becoming heroic himself, no small task.

Alexander, before he became "the Great," had certain advantages in forming himself and his destiny into an exception to the likes of Tokhtaymish. Alexander's father, King Philip of Macedon, saw to it that his son had a proper education, entrusting it to no less estimable a figure than the philosopher Aristotle. In Plutarch's account, Alexander learned the classics well: Along with a dagger, he kept the copy of the *Iliad* Aristotle had given him under his pillow every night as he was conquering the world. Likewise, Xenophon, in *Cyropedia*, described the education of Cyrus, which is at its core the story of the making of a hero capable of founding an empire in Persia.

One must note, however, the inherent instability of the Alexandrian solution to the problem of the hero in politics: Alexander died under mysterious circumstances at the age of 32. Poison was one possible explanation—an indication of the political peril to which even hero-kings were subject. And Machiavelli omits praise of Alexander in the same breath as Moses, Cyrus, Romulus, and Theseus. A conqueror-king, Alexander certainly was, and one of the most successful in history, a model for Julius Caesar (someone likewise absent from Machiavelli's admittedly incomplete list of the "most excellent"). But Alexander's conquest didn't last; he founded nothing.

For an encompassing portrait of classical elements of the hero as king, one can do little better than the epic of Gilgamesh, the oldest known story in the world, preceding the Hebrew Bible and the *Iliad* by about 1,000 years. The tale or series of tales of Gilgamesh comes to us in fragments, cuneiform tablets in Akkadian that lay undisturbed for centuries until their discovery in 1850. It would be decades longer before anyone was able to translate them. The contemporary man of letters and poet Stephen Mitchell, working from translations of the various fragments, published a compelling verse version of the story in 2004.

The historical Gilgamesh was the fifth king of Uruk, a city in modern Iraq that was arguably the apex of Sumerian civilization from the twenty-seventh through twenty-first centuries BCE. In the epic, the prowess of Gilgamesh is superhuman in scale, and he is said to be somehow two-thirds god and one-third human. Yet he remains throughout the tale distinctly human and mortal.

As the Mitchell version of the epic describes him:

> Surpassing all kings, powerful and tall
> beyond all others, violent, splendid,
> a wild bull of a man, unvanquished leader,
> hero in the front lines, beloved by his soldiers—
> *fortress* they called him, *protector of the people,*
> *raging flood that destroys all defenses.* . . .
> Who is like Gilgamesh? What other king
> has inspired such awe? Who else can say,
> "I alone rule, supreme among mankind?" (I)

Yet immediately after such encomia to his greatness comes the revelation that the rule of Gilgamesh is at least as tyrannical as it is kingly.

> He is king, he does whatever he wants,
> takes the son from his father and crushes him,
> takes the girl from her mother and uses her,
> the warrior's daughter, the young man's bride,
> he uses her, no one dares to oppose him. (I)

The people beseech the gods for relief from Gilgamesh's repressive propensity, and the response of the gods is to create:

a double for Gilgamesh, his second self,
a man who equals his strength and courage
a man who equals his stormy heart.
. . . a new hero, let them balance each other
perfectly, so that Uruk has peace. . . . (I)

Thus comes Enkidu, formed of the earth and literally a wild man, dropped by the gods in the wilderness to live absent contact with any human being. Eventually, a boy sees him in the wilderness and reports to Gilgamesh of the existence of this exotic creature. Gilgamesh is intrigued. He dispatches the temple priestess Shamhat, instructing her to use her "love-arts" to tame Enkidu. So she does: "For seven days / he stayed erect and made love with her, / until he had had enough" (I).

Enkidu is immensely strong. But his origin is that of a "natural" man. In the wild, he was free, the subject of no one. Only nature constrained him. He was entirely unschooled in the ways of human politics and rule by the strong, but at the same time he was entirely the master of himself. But Enkidu could not persist in this natural state, not after encountering the human love-artistry of Shamhat. (Rousseau, in his *Emile*, would go to great lengths in describing how a teacher might raise a child under the illusion that the only limitations on his freedom were those imposed by the natural world. This education would thereby approximate a benevolent natural condition, or state of nature, explicitly without the coercion of politics. Hence the famous problem at the center of Rousseau's political philosophy: "Man was born free, and he is everywhere in chains.")

When Shamhat tells Enkidu of the great king Gilgamesh, who she says is oppressing the people of Uruk, Enkidu's reaction is complicated. He vows to challenge the king to a fight to show that he, Enkidu, the naturally free man, is the mightiest: as it were, to strip Gilgamesh of the power and grandeur of his office and settle the matter naturally, by fighting. But at the same time, he is feeling something else, "a longing he had never known before, / the longing for a true friend" (I)

Shamhat tries to talk Enkidu out of challenging Gilgamesh. Yet when Enkidu hears from a passerby bridegroom the particulars of Gilgamesh's oppression, that he is about to enforce the *droit du seigneur* with the newest bride of Uruk, the passerby's own, Enkidu becomes outraged. He hastens to Uruk and stations himself in front of the bride's house, awaiting the arrival of the king. When Gilgamesh gets there, Enkidu makes good on his vow. They grapple at length, as the city itself shakes from the collisions of their epic battle. Finally, Gilgamesh prevails, pinning Enkidu and winning the latter's expression of acceptance of Gilgamesh as rightful king.

Gilgamesh the ruler of men has now met and contended with the naturally free man. Though the natural man has lost the contest, the willingness on the part of Enkidu to challenge him as no one else has ever done has provided Gilgamesh a glimpse of something he, too, has been missing: a friendship. Once Gilgamesh has Enkidu pinned, his anger dissipates.

This newly formed friendship is not grounded in equality any more than the relationship of Achilles and Patroclus is grounded in equality. If Enkidu refused to submit to the authority of Gilgamesh, Gilgamesh would have had no choice, one presumes, but to kill him. That Achilles is greater than Patroclus, or that Gilgamesh is greater than Enkidu, is a matter of agreement within each pair.

If the source of the profound affection Achilles feels for his greatest friend is elusive, perhaps Gilgamesh's equally profound affection for Enkidu illuminates both cases. Enkidu's challenge is a kind of first encounter on the part of Gilgamesh with someone who neither accedes in advance to his authority nor is simply a warring enemy to be slain. Once defeated, the challenger, who posed great difficulty and danger, is perhaps worthy of respect. The only way to demonstrate such respect, now and into the future, is to keep the challenger alive and show it. The people will observe and show their respect as well, but that's not really the point. The greatest hero has no need to recruit the esteem of others to the task of honoring his friend. The esteem of the hero is greater and more than sufficient honor. In constructing their relationship, the stronger and greater has elevated one other above all others, to the status of greatest friend.

The physical challenge of Enkidu to Gilgamesh may find its verbal analogue in Patroclus's reputation as a wise counselor to Achilles. In the end, the two greater figures make up their own minds about what they must do. But if Patroclus is anything more than a yes-man, which he certainly is, it can only be because he tells Achilles things Achilles doesn't want to hear. This, too, is a form of challenge. Achilles does not have to put up with such a challenge any more than Gilgamesh had to let Enkidu live. Each chooses to, however, for the sake of having a friend, the greatest friend.

Gilgamesh and Enkidu then set out together on an epic adventure, an account of the details of which is beyond our purpose here. Suffice it to say that in the course of winning their battles and deepening their personal bond, they manage to anger the gods. So it is that Enkidu, having suffered harrowing dreams he has interpreted as foretelling his doom, is beset by what seems to be a fever, and dies.

Gilgamesh grieves extravagantly, of course:

he tore out clumps of his hair, tore off
his magnificent robes as though they were cursed. (VIII)

The funeral is elaborate, more or less on par with that of Patroclus. Gilgamesh

... went to the treasury, unlocked the door
and surveyed his riches, then he brought out
priceless, jewel-studded weapons and tools,
with inlaid handles of ivory and gold,
and he heaped them up for Enkidu, his friend,
as an offering to the gods of the underworld.
He gathered fattened oxen and sheep,
... [etc.] (VIII)

But Gilgamesh has no human being to blame for the death of his friend, and therefore no vengeance to seek. A god has foretold that after burying Enkidu, Gilgamesh will "roam the wilderness / with matted hair, in a lion skin" (VII), which is to say, distraught and no longer interested in the fact or trappings of kingship—but, and the point is critical, no less great than he ever was. Gilgamesh is not a mere shadow of his former self. He is precisely his former self, "great in his greatness," one might say. The kingly rule and its perks and pleasures, though entirely appropriate to a figure so great, now stand revealed as mere accoutrements, incidental and unrelated to his personal obligation to fulfill his sense of inner greatness, now accompanied by the sense of having suffered the greatest possible loss.

From reflecting upon the death of his friend, Gilgamesh himself now reflects on his own fear of death:

"Must I die too? Must I be as lifeless
as Enkidu? How can I bear this sorrow
that gnaws at my belly, this fear of death
that restlessly drives me onward? . . . " (IX)

This is not the first time in the epic that Gilgamesh has expressed a fear of dying. He did so during the course of his adventure with Enkidu, and so did Enkidu. They variously talked each other into proceeding despite their fears. The point here (and throughout) is not that heroes are unafraid of death; it's that they overcome such fears and risk their lives despite them. Yet here, once again, is a reminder of the primal human longing for a type of being like that of the human but unencumbered by the burden of mortality.

Gilgamesh decides to act on this longing. He has heard the story of a man named Utnapishtim, whom the gods rewarded for his good services with eternal life:

". . . If only
I could find the one man whom the gods made immortal,
I would ask him how to overcome death." (IX)

So Gilgamesh sets out on another quest, this one less grand than his adventure with Enkidu. It takes him to the ends of the earth to find Utnapishtim.

It turns out that Utnapishtim was responsible for saving the human race. Certainly the greatest among many sensations the discovery of the *Gilgamesh* epic sparked arose from its account parallel to the Hebrew bible of the destruction of the world by a flood and its rebirth thanks to the willingness of a man, acting on advice from a god, to build a great boat to save himself along with his wife and the animals. Such was Utnapishtim's destiny.

When Gilgamesh reaches Utnapishtim at last, the king doesn't recognize the immortal. Gilgamesh is expecting the countenance and form of a god, but meets an old man instead. The latter tries to console him over the loss of Enkidu, noting that Gilgamesh's life has been a rich one, that all men must die but none knows when. Gilgamesh presses, and Utnapishtim recounts at length the story of the flood and the reward of immortality he received from the gods. He demands to know from Gilgamesh what comparable test the king is prepared to pass to earn such great favor from the gods. Gilgamesh, brought low in spirit by the death of his great friend, is now humbled, probably for the first time in his life, by this man-turned-immortal, a man whose achievement is greater than his own.

Utnapishtim proposes an initial test for Gilgamesh: Go for one week without sleeping. It's unclear whether Utnapishtim has the power to grant Gilgamesh the immortality he seeks; what is clear is that Utnapishtim knows Gilgamesh, bedraggled from his journey and exhausted from grief, cannot pass the test, and indeed, Gilgamesh falls asleep at once.

Yet before Utnapishtim sends Gilgamesh home, the immortal offers the king a consolation prize, an undersea plant that Utnapishtim says offers "the secret of youth" (XI).

It turns out the secret of youth is nothing other than an "antidote to the fear of death" (XI). It comes in the form of an underwater plant that Gilgamesh, following Utnapishtim's instructions, manages to locate beneath the sea. But Gilgamesh has hold of it only briefly before he loses it to the sea once again, with no possibility of finding it anew. Gilgamesh hasn't had time to try the antidote to the fear of death on himself. Apparently, he will never again cease to fear the fate that befell his great friend, as it befalls all human beings. Gilgamesh returns to Uruk and, in closing lines identical to the opening of the epic, recounts the grandeur of the city he rules.

Thus the great hero as great king. His happiness is incomplete in two ways, one capable of fulfillment, one impossible to fulfill. The great king needs a great friend, and he finds one. When his friend precedes him in death, the great king is overcome by the loss his friend's death represents and seeks immortality, which he cannot have. The only surcease from his newfound condition comes in the form of a chemically induced return to the mood of youth, a time of life when the possibility of death doesn't really come to mind. The young do not fear death because of their very youth.

Of course the young are incomplete as well; they are not yet the adults they will become. Precisely what they are missing is an awareness of the enormity of death. At a certain age, this comes to one. Some, such as Gilgamesh, overcome it through their willingness to risk their lives in fulfillment of their ambition and their inner sense of their own greatness. They leave monumental achievements in their wake—if not Uruk itself, the once-greatest city turned 4,000 years later entirely to dust, then the tale of Uruk and its king, recently recovered from the dust. Mortality makes the heroic possible.

## CHAPTER 4

# A HERO'S BARGAIN

*The attempt to tame the hero.*
*Settling for less than everything. Money and glory as rewards for valor.*
*The historical origin of "rights," first for the few,*
*in exchange for allegiance.*

If you are Alexander, to heroism born and bred, and are busy conquering the world, perhaps the danger posed by the heroic type does not bother you very much, so clear is your superiority over any potential rival. Even in such an extreme case, however, there is ample reason to be wary of complacency. We have noted the persistent bit of historical rumormongering holding that Alexander met his end by poison. Now, the figure of the poisoner is not exactly heroic in the mold of Achilles. The furtiveness and duplicity involved in the act seem to call for a separate category. Nevertheless, the act of poisoning the king is hardly risk-free, and the penalty for getting caught is indeed death.

We have so far been considering the hero as someone with a widely accepted claim to superiority, won in the ancient world by a willingness to risk death in service to the inner demands of greatness, perfection, or supreme ambition. Our category is accordingly somewhat formal: We have not delved much into the question of what constitutes *proper* ambition or how ambition might be improper; or what perfect virtue might consist of; or on what basis to distinguish great deeds from terrible deeds. The willingness to risk death in pursuit of improper ambition, or indeed in pursuit of perfect vice or of a "greatness" that is terrible, remains in our formal account a distinct possibility. The advantage of this approach, at least for now, is that it enables us to better understand superiority as such when it has come along. One and the same heroic type, for our purposes, can destroy a Republic *and* establish an Empire. Heroism is at the center of political creation as well as political destruction. Indeed, it is hard to imagine an act of political creation that has not entailed some form of political destruction, and until very recently, the process was almost always bloody.

So if you are in charge of the existing political order, whether you are king or tyrant or something else, you probably ought to be extraordinarily mindful of the danger the heroic type poses to the order you maintain. And this is true whether or not you, the king, are cut from an especially heroic cloth yourself.

Once one is alive to the danger, the logical next step is to think about ways to mitigate it. How does one keep the heroic type at bay?

Watching your back is one necessity that simple prudence dictates. As Hobbes noted, even the strongest person is vulnerable when sleeping. Physical security is a must, and it is not easy. Armed guards are probably necessary, but that leaves you with another problem, namely, guards with weapons, any one of whom might one day harbor the heroic (albeit treasonous) ambition to do in the king and take over his realm. *Quis custodiet ipsos custodes?* Who will watch the watchmen? The question describes a venerable and profound problem of political order.

We have heard Hiero, the tyrant of Syracuse, describe another method to reduce the risk of danger at the hands of the heroic type. He pursued a policy of preventive action: Identifying those sufficiently talented in one way or another to pose a potential threat, and then killing them before the threat had a chance to mature. Machiavelli has similar advice for a prince who has conquered another local principality: to hold on to it, one must "eliminate[] the line of the prince whose dominions they were" (III). In short, off with the children's and nephews' heads. The maintenance of political order in the face of the danger the classical hero poses is not for the squeamish.

Consider the troubling case of Joan of Arc and her relation to Charles VII, who would become king of France thanks largely to Joan. Joan heard voices, which she interpreted as coming from God. This was not an everyday phenomenon even in the fourteenth century. Joan also had a distinctly un–fourteenth-century penchant for dressing as a man. She was, in a word, strange for her time. But her voices were telling her to kick the English out of France and restore the dauphin to the throne, and she had an amazing ability to lead soldiers to victory in battle. This led to a certain indulgence for her peculiarities on the part of those who sought to benefit from this most unlikely of military heroes, first and foremost the dauphin. And so it was that England suffered humiliating defeats and Charles VII had his coronation in Reims.

Joan sought to drive the English from France because that's what God wanted her to do. This is a religious version of the cultivation of one's inner sense of greatness or perfection. Joan acted in the service of no one, except, as she saw it, God. She was not acting on behalf of Charles; he was an incidental beneficiary, possessor of rightful title to the throne upon her success in her God-given mission.

Unfortunately for Joan, the English captured her. In ordinary circumstances, a prisoner would be eligible for ransoming. Joan's family didn't have any money, but more to the point, Charles VII never lifted a finger on her behalf. We are left to speculate about the motive underlying his decision. Well, who knew what Joan's voices would tell her to do next? From Charles's point of view, instruction from voices beyond the influence of anyone else—in fact, inaudible to anyone else—cannot have looked like a dependable source of wise counsel for someone with the capacity to take up arms and lead soldiers into battle.

Charles seems to have been content to pocket the fruits of Joan's heroism and let the English take care of whatever problem she might subsequently pose for him. So the English burned her at the stake on dubious charges of heresy. Joan reportedly accepted her martyrdom with panache, since she knew that far from being a heretic, she had acted according to God's wishes as personally conveyed to her. Her conduct was, in her own eyes, above reproach. As for Charles VII, history does not definitively record whether he was at all bothered by his betrayal of his deliverer. But clearly, he did well for himself. He became known as Charles le Victorieux, Charles the Victorious. Not bad—though the French also called him Charles le Bien-Servi, Charles the Well-Served, which perhaps captures his good fortune a little better: a *hero* served him.

But armed guards, timely murder, and betrayal are not the only avenues of security available to the forces of political order in their attempts to mitigate heroic danger. There is also the possibility of working to try to modify the heroic type as such. That burning ambition, that cultivation of perfection, that sense of greatness itching from within, that sense of self as the chosen vehicle of divine being for working its will in the world—perhaps there is some way to give it satisfaction short of a resolution calling for the complete disruption of the status quo.

In particular, perhaps there is some way to take an initially inner-driven passion and turn it inside-out—to gather elements of the forces of political order to scratch the heroic itch to its own satisfaction before it can endanger political order. It would be an exercise in trying to take a hero's inner-directed sense of greatness and make it other-directed—that is, satisfied by *others'* recognition of the fact of greatness and the rightness of the claim to superiority.

I think Pompey the Great is broadly representative of the heroic type finding satisfaction in this way. Of Pompey's willingness to risk his life, there can be no doubt. He was a conqueror of the first order. But he was also a proud and leading Roman citizen. He felt vested in the political order that was the Roman Republic—so much so that he would be the

Republic's last resort in its futile attempt to stave off ruin at the hands of Julius Caesar. Why?

No small part of the answer to this question must be: because the Republic bestowed honors upon such heroic individuals as Pompey. The Romans had a special knack for this kind of reward, on both a small and large scale.

The Romans were pioneers in the granting of medals for meritorious conduct in wartime. The *torc* was a gold neckpiece. *Armillae* were gold armbands. *Phalerae* were disks of gold, silver, or bronze worn on the breastplate of one's armor on ceremonial occasions. The francophone twentieth-century philosopher Alexandre Kojève, drawing on Hegel, would remark on the importance of the desire for "recognition" of one's status as a superior type, in this case a willingness to risk one's life for a mere scrap of cloth or metal—a military decoration. Militaries have long kept order and discipline in the ranks not only by a set of punishments for misbehavior but also by largely symbolic rewards for excellence. This tradition continues to this day—though, as we shall see in Chapter 8, the standards of excellence have changed.

As we have noted in Caesar's case, a great conquering general returning to Rome could expect a triumph, a vast processional, ceremony, and feast in which he became a demigod for the day. In the third century BCE, the contemporary historian Livy records, when Marcus Claudius Marcellus came back to Rome after conquering Sicily, he entered the city as part of a massive parade in his honor, including his soldiers, their war engines, his prisoners, the treasure he had ransacked, as well as eight elephants.

Pompey the Great had three triumphs, each more extravagant than the preceding. They honored his victories in Africa, Hispania, and the East, where the territories ruled by several major local kings, including Jerusalem, became Roman provinces thanks to his knack for conquest and subjugation. It is no small thing to have the sobriquet "the Great" appended to your name in your own lifetime. Coriolanus got his honorific name as a result of his victory over the Volscians at Corioli. Likewise,

Scipio became Africanus for doing very well as a general on the far side of the Mediterranean. Not bad. But it's not nearly as good as the straight-forwardly comprehensive "Pompey the Great." It is uncertain whether he spoke of himself as "I, Pompey the Great," but he seems to have been a stranger to all humility, including the false sort.

Of course, in addition to glory there was money. Pompey was not the richest man in Rome at the time; that distinction belonged to Crassus, who also won Roman honors for his generalship. Crassus won the charge to suppress the slave revolt led by the former gladiator Spartacus. On his way back to Rome after successfully doing so, Crassus had a slave crucified on the roadside of the Via Appia about every quarter mile, leaving the corpses hanging to rot post-mortem as a warning to others. The man had a certain anti-panache; in addition to his spectacular cruelty, noteworthy even by the standards of the day, there was his relish in exploiting fellow Roman citizens in moments of weakness for the sake of personal gain. A significant part of his great fortune came from buying at rock-bottom prices from desperate owners properties in town that had caught fire or were in danger of doing so. He would then send in a team of specially trained slaves to put the fire out. Those property owners who declined to sell got no firefighting assistance, of course; Crassus's fire brigade was not a charitable enterprise. Most people then and now consider greed to be a self-centered quality, and for the most part, this is so. But for our purposes, we should note that if pecuniary rewards were sufficient to fulfill the ambition of a Crassus, then Roman political order was the beneficiary. Money is a social commodity, and the desire to acquire it is accordingly other-directed in a way that heroic inner greatness of the highest type is not.

Though he was no Crassus, Pompey had more wealth than he needed for the finest things in life then available, and enough besides to shower great largess on Rome proper, most notably by building a grand theater that would bear his name, an architectural tribute to himself. Again, the desire to erect such a structure, though grandiose, is resolutely other-directed, designed to make people think well of one indefinitely, if not quite forever.

The taming of Pompey, if one may speak in such terms, was not the clever stratagem of a wary king who saw the heroic danger Pompey posed and moved to counteract it. Rather, it was a product of Pompey's rootedness in Rome, of his sense of vestiture in the Republic. As "the Great" in his own eyes, he deserved the great wealth of the conqueror, the esteem of the best and most prominent of his contemporaries, and the highest honors. But these rewards from others were enough for him. His ambition could be satisfied within the context of the political order in which he grew up. He didn't need to remake it. One could properly say that the routine satisfaction of great political ambition *within* an existing political order is a mark of its strength and stability, now no less than then. Pompey *contributed* to that political order without an apparent second thought. He was prepared to risk his life not out of a superordinate inner drive to express greatness but in return for the rewards, tangible and intangible, that a prominent Roman could expect in exchange for a willingness to take on Rome's enemies—thus *for Rome*.

But the political order of the late Roman Republic was insufficient to turn all itches of inner greatness outward in pursuit of a scratching post. It did not tame Julius Caesar, and all it took to destroy the Republic was one exception. In the end, the shape the Republic's political order imparted to Pompey turned out to be insufficient to allow him to restore the old order by defeating Caesar's challenge to it. In Caesar's view, Pompey had the opportunity but failed to seize it: "Today victory had been with the enemy, if they had had a victor in command." Was Pompey, in the end, too tame, and the Republican political order that tamed him accordingly too vulnerable, to a challenge from a heroic type unmoored to it, a Caesar? I find the answer here elusive and the question haunting, because this question for Rome is also a question for our time, as we shall see in the final chapter.

How do you go about getting people, including the heroic types, vested in the existing political order, therefore aborting any inclination on their part to conclude that the existing political order is no match for their superiority and must be overthrown?

We have been describing the classical hero as an ideal type. Such a hero is heroic not *on behalf of* something (such as the people) but as the outward expression of a felt sense of superiority or greatness. The praise of the people is what the hero subsequently receives, but it is not something an Achilles seeks. The instances in which heroes switch sides on their people illustrate this fundamental absence of connection. The politics of classical heroism goes little beyond a demonstration of superiority against all comers.

Yet the greater number of instances in which heroes do not switch sides, but remain with and loved by their people, remind us that the hero's assertion of superiority often has profound political consequences. As we have seen, sometimes a hero ends up founding a great religion or a state, for example, or taking one over, or saving one from being taken over. The hero then ends up linked to that state in a way that obscures the diremption between the hero's aspiration and any aspirations that other, lesser persons may have for their hero: to make heroism useful to them. If our hero founded our state, it was not an activity undertaken for us, although we are the beneficiaries.

It is certainly possible to imagine a slightly different sort of character, heroic in the sense of willing to risk death to achieve great deeds that win the acclaim of the people, but with the great deeds serving some other purpose than outward manifestation of inner greatness. The hero could, in short, have aspirations on behalf of the people, or the state, or the god(s) the hero and the people share. Heroic ambition in the classical sense could be constrained and modified by being made subservient to some greater cause than the hero's own, specifically, in one form or another, the state or the aspirations for a state.

The problem of the collision of heroism and politics found a path to resolution when political authorities figured out how to put a hero to use in service of their ends. Ultimately, the test of the success of this resolution, the domestication of heroism through its subordination to politics, has depended on the willingness of heroic types to be content with something less than total political power—or perhaps to be content with something other than the overthrow of existing political power. Political authorities have often worked hard to foster this contentment, which could offer some protection from the manifest danger greatness might pose to them. Their chief means have been two: money and glory. They have heaped riches and accolades on the heroic types in their midst in the hope that enjoyment of these external rewards would discourage heroics of the sort that might pose a political danger. This is more or less the position in which every glorious Roman conqueror found himself, and usually it was sufficient to provide satisfaction, Caesar once again the exception.

The martial virtues would certainly entail a certain fearlessness about fighting, a willingness to risk death. But for what, exactly? Now, not so much for the pursuit of unquenchable personal ambition. But for the good of the Crown, for the honor of a noble house (one's own), for the sake of a political and social order in which one enjoyed a lofty place, for glory and the esteem of one's peers, for the personal pleasure of killing one's enemies.

Clearly, something of the classically heroic remains here. Equally clearly, not all. The willingness to risk death remains, as does an inner sense of obligation to oneself and one's superior qualities. But in the case of the aristocracy, and unlike the cases of Achilles, Lucretia, or Julius Caesar, the interior obligation has been socialized, has obtained direction from outside. It's the perfection of oneself in an accepted *role*. And from the point of view of the king, it's a role assigned and cultivated by the king for the good of the king.

When the legendary King Arthur of fifth- or sixth-century England convened his court, according to the old stories, he famously constituted the warrior-barons around him as "the Knights of the Round Table." The first such description of the Round Table dates to the eleventh century.

The roundness of the table is of considerable interest here. The point Arthur was said to be making with his table was that he, though king, would not choose to lord it over the knights. The Round Table was a sign of respect for them and for their prerogatives. He would not position himself at the head of a table, as *their* head, as though he could command them without taking into consideration their wishes. Nor would he have to assign them a rank in relation to one another, in descending order down the table from the king. Thus we have a correlative of feudal and chivalric order in the very furniture of the Court.

By all accounts, Arthur was a wise king. But we might want to pause a moment rather than accept at face value the propaganda on his behalf. There really isn't the slightest indication of equality of any sort around the Round Table. The king was still the king, round or square be his table; he knew it, and the barons knew it. What's more, it seems rather undeniable that Arthur had his favorites among the knights: Sir Kay, Sir Bedivere, Sir Gawain. Early visual depictions of the Round Table usually show a special spot reserved for King Arthur, and even if not, it's a pretty good bet that wherever the king chose to sit, there resided pride of place. Nor was it likely irrelevant who sat closest to the king, at his right and left hand. It seems unlikely in the extreme that Arthur and his court actually saw themselves as a company of equals, or even Arthur as somehow "first among equals" (whatever that means).

Nevertheless, it's not hard to see why the Round Table was good for kingly business. It cost Arthur nothing to pay this bit of respect to his barons, and in doing so, he advanced an objective of keen interest to his ability to retain his crown. He reduced (without quite eliminating) the propensity for infighting among knights jockeying for place within the kingdom.

Such infighting would be severely disadvantageous to the king. First, if the barons set to warring among themselves, they might be unavailable to the king for such tasks as repelling the Saxons, conquering Gaul, and seeking the Holy Grail. Worse, such infighting might well end not in a stalemate reinforcing the status quo, but in a victorious baron more powerful than all the others. This would seem to be a recipe for the creation of a capable pretender to the king's throne.

Instead, the Round Table served to guarantee the status of each of the barons as, in effect, personally protected by the king. They were equals, of a kind, in the enjoyment of this status—which is to say, they were equals in their subservience to the king. Any desire on the part of one to challenge the status of another would directly contravene the political order the king imposed. It would not be a test of baron versus baron, but of baron versus crown, since the king could not allow such a challenge to his authority to go forward with impunity. Such a challenge would be treasonous, warranting death.

The Arthurian bargain offered his barons security against each other by transforming any such contest into a challenge to the authority of the crown. But wouldn't that seem to broaden the danger to the crown, turning any passing dispute among knights into an existential political crisis in which the king must restore order on his own terms or face the collapse of his authority? Not really. The problem of the authority of the king was omnipresent, as we have seen, subject at all times to disruption by the emergence of someone of the heroic type. Arthur found a way to deter the underlying conflict through his Round Table, thereby diminishing the likelihood of the emergence of the heroic type. Knights would fight battles in service to the king, but among themselves, they would participate not in mortal struggle but only in the mock combat of what came to be known in the later Middle Ages as "Roundtable Games." In short, they would joust. I imagine that kings always looked on approvingly when the individuals who potentially posed the greatest threat to their person and their crown were jousting.

The Arthur legend, properly construed, offers a fairly thorough phenomenological account of the origin of feudal order and the birth of chivalry. Feudalism was a kingly attempt to solve the problem of political instability at the hands of the heroic type—an attempt to tame the hero. To the extent it worked, it did so by granting something like "rights" to a group of already powerful individuals in the hope that these kingly privileges would be sufficient to satisfy their ambition.

Just as kings propounded law not only to honor their gods and to serve their people, but also to make the task of ruling more regular and predictable, demarcating what would and would not constitute a challenge to their authority, so they came to understand the advantages of a lawful privileged class and to codify those privileges.

In this respect, Moses got some excellent advice from his father-in-law Jethro. After leading the Israelites out of Egypt and Pharoah's clutches, Moses was feeling beset. His people were calling upon him from dawn to dusk to settle disputes among themselves by telling them God's will. Jethro saw that this was just too much for his son-in-law:

> [Jethro] said to him, "The thing that you are doing is not good. You will surely wear out, both yourself and these people who are with you, for the task is too heavy for you; you cannot do it alone. Now listen to me: I will give you counsel, and God be with you. You be the people's representative before God, and you bring the disputes to God, then teach them the statutes and the laws, and make known to them the way in which they are to walk and the work they are to do. Furthermore, you shall select out of all the people able men who fear God, men of truth, those who hate dishonest gain; and you shall place *these* over them *as* leaders of thousands, of hundreds, of fifties and of tens. Let them judge the people at all times; and let it be that every major dispute they will bring to you, but every minor dispute they themselves will judge. So it will be easier for you, and they will bear *the burden* with you. If you do this thing and God *so* commands you, then you will be able to endure, and all these people also will go to their place in peace." (Exodus 18:17–23)

Hitherto and subsequently in Exodus, we read about God laying down the law for Moses. But as far as determining how to organize a stiff-necked people so that they can operate in accordance with the law, this is a task for man.

In the terms of the selection criteria for this hierarchy of civil admin-istration, Jethro places the emphasis on competence and then virtue: able men who are god-fearing and truthful and hate injustice. These sound remarkably like men with the qualities that our tyrant Hiero, when he identified them, slew preemptively; that's one solution. But another is Jethro's strategy of cooptation, which Moses pursued to good effect. As Moses's admirer Machiavelli notes:

> the first conjecture that is to be made of the brain of a lord is to see the men he has around him; and when they are capable and faithful, he can always be reputed wise because he has known how to recognize them as capable and to maintain them as faithful. (XXII)

One gets a similar sense of the problem of political adversaries and the potential for taming them from the experience of King John in early thirteenth-century England. John's assumption of the throne in 1199 was itself a highly problematic affair. The succession was in dispute, the law supposedly governing it differing within the realm itself. Should the crown of Richard the Lionheart pass to his brother John, as the sole surviving son of Henry II? Or did it rightfully belong to Arthur of Brittany, the son of John's late older brother Geoffrey? For our purposes, we can merely note that the crown is, indeed, worth a fight, at least for a certain kind of person. It's good to be the king. But it's also difficult and dangerous.

John initially enjoyed the allegiance of most of the nobles in Eng-land and Normandy, whereas Arthur's claim was favored among most continental barons and by Philip II, the French king, whose ambition it was to kick the English back across the channel. In the event, John was crowned in London, but the struggle for control of the French part of what has come to be called the Angevin empire was well under way. During his tenure in office, John fought for but ultimately lost his pos-sessions in Normandy and other continental territory, leaving him with only the Duchy of Aquitaine there. Above all, he wanted Normandy back, and he undertook extensive and expensive military preparations and campaigns to attempt to regain it in the decade following its loss, all without success.

This rankled the aristocracy. The expense of his exactions in support of his futile campaign and the loss of continental possessions (as well as an additional bit of unpleasantness concerning John's capitulation to the demands of Pope Innocent III) combined to kindle a rebellion among the barons in England's North and East. To head it off, John started to negotiate, certainly in bad faith, on protections for the prerogatives of the barons in case of dispute with the crown. He affixed his seal to a package of reforms in 1215, which seemed to placate the barons at least briefly. But John never had any intention of abiding by the terms of the deal, which included among other fanciful provisions the establishment of a 25-member council of barons that could hold the King to account by seizing his property if he violated the deal's terms. To get out of the pact more gracefully, John subsequently sent to Pope Innocent III to secure a pronouncement that this bargain with the barons violated John's kingly prerogatives, as well as John's (nominal) allegiance to the pope as his feudal lord. Once the pope started excommunicating the barons, the situation quickly became one of open rebellion, which would preoccupy John until his death a year later.

Now, admittedly, my description in the previous paragraphs is not how people usually tell the story of the *Magna Carta*—for such is the story I was telling. Generally, there is a great deal of high sentence to the tale, an account of the initial flourishing of the rights of the English people, won over and against the power of an abusive king. And indeed, the *Magna Carta* is a great historical document, not so much for what it did at the time as for what subsequent generations made it into, a kind of foundational document for political rights.

The *Magna Carta* does indeed, in its first chapter, proffer the king's guarantee of "all the liberties underwritten" to "all the free men of Our kingdom." A similar formulation occurs in the last chapter, 63: "all men in Our Kingdom shall have and hold all the aforesaid liberties, rights, and concessions, well and peaceably, freely, quietly, fully, and wholly, to them and their heirs, of Us and Our heirs, in all things and places forever, as is aforesaid." One of its provisions, Chapter 39, also bears a likeness to latter-day concerns about ensuring the rule of law and due process of law: "No free man shall be taken, imprisoned, disseised [dispossessed of property], outlawed, banished, or in any way destroyed, nor will We proceed against or prosecute him, except by the lawful judgment of his peers and by the law of the land." A quasi-"equal protection" guarantee follows immediately in Chapter 40: "To no one will We deny or delay, right or justice."

The language of these provisions, among others, certainly figured prominently in subsequent efforts to render protections of the kind specified in the *Magna Carta* actual, as opposed to notional. In later instances in which royal power seemed overweening, critics explicitly invoked the promises of the *Magna Carta* in their demands for relief. This was intermittently effective. And indeed, modern history is replete with instances in which authoritarian rulers made false promises only to run into serious complexity and danger when people started using their own words against them. The use of the human rights provisions of the 1974 Helsinki Accords became a lever against the would-be totalitarian governments of the Soviet Union and its Warsaw Pact allies.

Nevertheless, in the context of 1215, the *Magna Carta* is better understood as an attempt on the part of a beset king to pacify rebellious aristocrats by paying lip-service to their demands with guarantees for their prerogatives against the Crown. One way to look at this is that John acceded to their demands, or at least said he was doing so. Another and better interpretation, I think, is that the barons were acceding to the king's demands: that John, in possession of supreme kingly power, persuaded them to give up their rebellion against him merely by seeming to grant them their claims. He won peace not by fighting and defeating the barons, but by affixing his seal to a piece of paper, after which they went home.

True, John's victory over them didn't hold. Would it have, had John's intention been to honor the provisions of the document he agreed to? Could he have tamed the barons permanently by upholding his promises in the Great Charter?

On one hand, it seems unlikely. Their grievances against an unsuccessful king were broad and deep. On the other hand, the barons were not an especially impressive lot. It's noteworthy, for example, that the contretemps surrounding the *Magna Carta* goes by the name of the First Barons' War, and not by the name of anyone who participated in it. Robert Fitzwalter was its leader, but a household name he is not. And in fact one of the chief problems the barons had in their halfhearted effort to oust their lawful sovereign was their inability to settle among themselves on a suitable pretender to the throne. To me, this suggests that rather than the *Magna Carta* taming the powers of the king (or paving the way to curtailment of kingly power), or the king taming the barons through the false promises of the *Magna Carta*, the *Magna Carta* was a document that reflected an already-tamed baronial class, more interested in the preservation of its own privileges than in heroic aspiration to seize the crown.

Feudal order was hardly proof against the emergence of a politically disruptive heroic type. Succession to the throne was the political problem par excellence, and disputed claims often turned into epic struggles, as in the Wars of the Roses, the 32-year battle for the crown between the House of York and the House of Lancaster in the fifteenth century, among many other such struggles. Yet it was only rarely the case that a baron with no remotely plausible claim to the throne sought to fight and maneuver his way to the supreme prize, and only the controversial Oliver Cromwell who achieved it.

The barons were, over the centuries and in general, nobody's cowards. They fought for their king against enemies abroad, and they took sides in fights over the crown itself at home. Risk of life was never far from their pursuits. Yet they were almost always more vested in the existing political order than they were out to upset it in order to obtain supreme control. They were hard men, but within limits. You wouldn't want to cross one, but a king could regard most of them as tame enough to pose no serious threat.

Nevertheless, history is replete with instances in which serving the crown or state was not enough. Napoleon stood in a long line of generals whose ambition and sense of their own prowess combined with a status close enough to the pinnacle of political power for them to envision grasping it for themselves. Political authorities who successfully domesticated their generals were sometimes still at risk from the echelon below. It is no accident that colonels, such as Libyan strongman Muammar Qaddafi, have figured so prominently in coup d'état attempts around the world. Coup plotters have often perceived their immediate superior officers to have grown weak and complacent owing to excessive exposure to the largess and encomiums of the political powers-that-be. There, they have found opportunity.

But failure in the attempt to tame those inclined to heroic deeds has not been inevitable. The United States military and the military establishments of other modern states stand as proof that under certain circumstances, a relationship of subordination of the military to political authority can be stable, accepted by both politicians and generals. Even here, however, the long-standing difficulty inherent in the relationship between political authority and military power occasionally rears up in a fashion that requires serious attention at the highest levels.

The notion of senior members of the U.S. military plotting a coup against the civil authorities was once a staple of popular fiction and Hollywood films. *Seven Days in May*, in book (1962) and movie (1964) version, is probably the classic of the genre. Set in the early 1970s, the movie features Burt Lancaster as an ambitious Joint Chiefs Chairman outraged at the president's decision to sign a nuclear weapons deal with the Soviet Union in which both sides will dismantle their arsenals. He and the other service chiefs, complicit with hawkish opponents of the White House in Congress, launch a plot to oust the president and take over the country. The coup gets foiled largely thanks to an intrepid colonel

(Kirk Douglas), who, though himself an opponent of the president's plan, is outraged at the prospect of the overthrow of the U.S. Constitution.

The plot of *Seven Days in May* is fanciful in the usual manner of Hollywood and the thriller genre of fiction. It is not "realistic." Yet I think it does offer a keen insight into the problem of civil-military relations and the extent to which the United States and other classically liberal, constitutional democracies have largely resolved this problem.

Stipulate, for purposes of argument, that a Joint Chiefs Chairman might secretly harbor Bonapartist tendencies. What would be the chance of successfully acting on them, and why? I say quite low, for one reason familiar to us from our consideration of past efforts to tame the heroic type, and for one reason somewhat more recent in origin.

The first is the example of Pompey, who was no threat to the Roman Republic but rather its last hope. He was loyal through and through, down to the end. Why? I don't think Pompey's loyalty was the product solely of Rome's egregious official flattery—being dubbed "the Great." Rather, it was the connectedness Pompey felt to Rome altogether. He found in Rome a container that held and rewarded the full measure of his ambition. Caesar, of course, did not. American generals and their modern counterparts reap considerable rewards in terms of prestige and (after they retire) money from their service to and allegiance to their country. They have also scaled the heights of a demanding profession. The political system, meanwhile, remains open to them should they be inclined to enter the partisan fray (though top-echelon military commanders have only rarely chosen to go into electoral politics, Dwight Eisenhower being the successful exception and former top NATO commanders Al Haig and Wesley Clark the unsuccessful exceptions).

Meanwhile, the constitutional tradition of civilian control, with the president as commander in chief, seems thoroughly ingrained at all levels of the military. This factor works profoundly against acting on the factual stipulation with which we began, namely an impulse to take over the country.

We can see how strong the principle of civilian control is even in the breach. General Stanley McChrystal was President Barack Obama's top commander in Afghanistan in 2010 when a magazine article appeared quoting senior members of his staff, in his presence, making disparaging remarks about the president and senior administration officials. Obama promptly recalled McChrystal to Washington and accepted his resignation. Even many admirers of McChrystal's considerable talent as a warrior, as well as many people critically disposed toward the president, supported the general's ouster on grounds that the public display of disrespect was intolerable. Yet I note that this was hardly a matter of insubordination, let alone a precursor to a coup. Members of the military from the top down have always had opinions about politics and politicians. Mostly, they keep them to themselves, especially at senior levels. The cause of McChrystal's removal was indiscretion, the point being that so much as the expression of disrespect is a firing offense, given well-settled expectations with regard to civilian control of the military.

A second reason to doubt the prospects of success of a *Seven Days in May*–style coup is one the plot itself points to: It's the colonel. Service members are also citizens of a modern democratic polity. I imagine that like most citizens in general, most of them are mostly content in the broadest sense with contemporary political arrangements. Notwithstanding low approval ratings in public opinion surveys for Congress and the president, no one much seems to harbor an inclination for ditching the constitutional system and replacing it with a monarchy or a dictatorship. I don't think the reason for this is merely fear of the consequences of unsuccessful revolution. Indeed, the most radical critics of our politics these days argue explicitly in terms of a *return* to the basic principles of the Constitution, not for overthrowing it or even overhauling it.

Given high social satisfaction with existing political arrangements, a satisfaction whose prevalence extends fully into the citizen-soldier ranks of the U.S. military, our notional renegade Joint Chiefs chairman would find himself in a difficult position, though one not unfamiliar to plotters of coups from time immemorial: To the extent the plot hinges on the participation of others, the effort to recruit them vastly increases the risk of exposure by someone more attached to existing political arrangements than enamored of the possibilities of a new order. The colonels are more likely to take action to blow the whistle and save the republic than to attach themselves to the supreme aggrandizement of somebody else's ambition.

What they serve now, a modern egalitarian republic whose citizens are rights-bearing individuals like themselves, is superior to the comprehensive subservience they would owe to a successful coup leader. Indeed, their willingness to take risks to defend the existing order would constitute a type of heroism we will take up more fully beginning in Chapter 8. Meanwhile, though, it is time to look at some of the characteristics of a modern, egalitarian republic.

## CHAPTER 5

# HEROISM AND DEMOCRACY

*Superiority versus equality.*
*The leveling tendency of egalitarian society.*
*Fascism as a repudiation of equality.*

Modernity is very much a work in progress. Political conditions in much of today's world—though not everywhere, of course—aren't all that different from the general political conditions of two or three thousand years ago. The world today is home to a number of weak or failed states where central governmental authority has collapsed. In these spaces, we can still get a glimpse of the Hobbesian pregovernmental state of nature and "the war of every man against every man." Such order as obtains usually comes from a strongman or warlord who is first of all concerned with the preservation of his own position of superiority. Such a warlord probably has a set of lieutenants whom he relies on to maintain his position, but whose loyalty is a concern of the first magnitude for the warlord. These are the nodes of today's world in which heroism in the classical and formal sense, the willingness to risk life in order to assert superiority, is still readily in play.

But, of course, this is hardly the totality of the political condition of today's world. Much of the modern world is democratic in character.

Governments function reasonably well and are limited in scope, leaving a wide swath of human activity minimally regulated or unregulated, and therefore perpetuating conditions of freedom. Governments are rights-regarding: they respect human rights, civil rights, political rights. The way to settle disputes between individuals is not a fight or duel or feud, but peaceably, if necessary with recourse to mediators, arbitrators, or the courts. The way to settle policy questions is through the action of legislators, officials of the administrative state, and sometimes (when the question involves the basic law of the state) the courts. Although governments have coercive authority at their disposal, most people willingly accept as binding these legislative enactments, administrative regulations, and court rulings.

The way to settle who decides policy questions is through periodic free and fair elections, in which the victor is the one with the most votes. What makes the elections free and fair is that the contenders seek or obtain no illegal or illegitimate advantage over their opponents. What's more, the losers enjoy broad protections, including the protection of their rights against the caprice of the majority, as well as the ability to contest the next election. An election does not establish a permanent winner who can rightly claim all available spoils, but rather a temporary outcome subject to reversal.

Perhaps most striking of all, mature democratic states in the modern world seem readily able to avoid violent conflict with one another. Such disputes as they have, they are willing to settle peacefully. Their "vital interests" never seem to come into conflict in a way that would entail a test of arms. This phenomenon, anticipated by the German philosopher Immanuel Kant in his essay "Perpetual Peace," goes by the name of the "democratic peace." The empirical fact of a democratic peace is widely accepted, though there is no consensus on the explanation for it. Somehow, the internal character of the regime must tell us something about how it will interact with regimes of like character. This in turn suggests a level of commonality above that of the supreme political entity, the state. We, the citizens of a democratic state, regard the citizens of other democratic states as "like us," much the way we regard the residents of our own country as like us. At home, peace obtains not solely because of a powerful central government willing and able to use its monopoly on the legitimate use of force to enforce its decrees, à la Hobbes and other thinkers of the "realist" stripe, but also because people are peaceably inclined toward others "like us." The same principle appears to translate with regard to others "like us" abroad.

Alexis de Tocqueville, the great chronicler of both nineteenth-century America and the dawning democratic age, would perhaps have little difficulty with the notion of "others like us" extending beyond national borders. He thought that the notion of one's *semblables* was a distinctly new one in politics, directly traceable to the passion for equality driving democracy not only in America but likewise, and no less inexorably, in the Old World of Europe, where kings and nobles still ruled the roost.

Tocqueville takes as his subject the entry and subsequent domination of this spirit of equality into a world whose politics for centuries was aristocratic in character:

> as I studied American society, more and more I saw in equality of conditions the generative fact from which each particular fact seemed to issue, and I found it before me constantly as the central point at which all my observations came to an end.
>
> Then I brought my thinking back to our hemisphere [that is, Europe], and it seemed to me I distinguished something in it analogous to the spectacle the New World offered me. I saw the equality of conditions that, without having reached the its extreme limits as it had in the United States, was approaching them each day; and the same democracy reigning in American societies appeared to me to be advancing rapidly toward power in Europe. (3)

For Tocqueville, "equality of conditions" was not a fact merely of political life, the underpinning of a democratic form of government but little more. On the contrary, the egalitarianism was at the center of what Tocqueville called the "social state" (45–53), which comprises not just political arrangements but also the manners and morals of society as a whole.

The old aristocratic order was going, going, if not yet gone. Since the Middle Ages, political order had been centered on hereditary property-owners—the aristocracy—and its members' obligations on the one hand to their sovereign and on the other to those living on their land (who in turn understood they were obliged to their noble lord). We have seen how the establishment of this aristocratic class offers a potential solution to the age-old problem of the classical hero's potentially destabilizing effect on political order—why self-imposed limits on sovereign power might be in the interest of the sovereign. If it's possible to buy off many or most potential rivals for supreme power with heritable titles of nobility and permanent grants of land along with the riches that ensue, why not try? It may be an imperfect or partial solution, but in a game of thrones there really isn't anything better.

Now, however, it's time to take with Tocqueville the next step, to mark with him the arrival of the spirit of equality. The colonists of the New World were hardly bereft of strong leaders, or a sense of rank among themselves. But they were not vassals, and they had no lords, not in the manner of the Old World and its hereditary nobility. The king of England had his representatives on the scene, the colonial governors, who along with their subsidiary officials were responsible for public administration, taxes for the Crown, and the like. But these officials, powerful though they were, were not barons and dukes, and the Americans knew it.

The feudal aristocracy of the Old World was relatively stable for the centuries in which both the nobility and the people accepted it as an almost organic condition of political life, perhaps mandated by heaven as the only worldly alternative to turmoil and upheaval. We have seen what a contrivance feudal order actually is: the partial empowerment of the few by the one to try to prevent the emergence of a rival one. But for those who were following the life-paths laid out by their grandparents' grandparents—and doing so, moreover, in hope of eternal salvation, a cause that would not be furthered by disobedience to one's lawful lord—the existing order of political arrangements may have been debatable on the merits but was certainly deemed unavoidable.

In the New World, however, there were no baronial intermediaries between the people and their king. The relationship, though remote in distance, was more direct. Moreover, there was no Church authority buttressing the existing order through threats of eternal damnation for acts of rebellion. In England from the time of the Magna Carta, "the people" obtained rights mostly through the assertion of aristocratic privilege against the power of the Crown—a highly consequential but nevertheless collateral benefit, the privileges of the nobility being the nobility's first concern, as the privileges of the Crown were the Crown's first concern. The New World colonists asserted their rights directly, including a right to rebel against a repressive king.

Thomas Hobbes is generally known as the supreme philosophical defender of sovereign power. But he, too, was writing in an age of aristocracy. Tellingly, his *Leviathan* cuts out the middlemen, the nobility, to center governance on the relationship of the people and their desires on one hand and the sovereign who protects them from the "war of every man against every man" on the other. I doubt that Hobbes would have thought the American colonists made an especially persuasive case, in their July 4, 1776 Declaration of Independence, for the necessity of rebellion against their lawful sovereign, at least based on the catalogue of the misdeeds of George III the document enumerates. Nevertheless, Hobbes would have been pleased, I think, for he ascribed to the people exactly this right of revolution in case of an abrogation of the sovereign's responsibility. In *Leviathan* as an unstated theoretical prerequisite and in America in fact, the absence of a class of nobility created an unmediated relationship between the people and the king that was quite different from the norm of eighteenth-century Europe.

This unmediated relationship turned out to be good for the people and not so good for the king, who lost his colonies (though not his crown, nor his head). The absence of an aristocratic class is one of the principal differences distinguishing the American Revolution from the French Revolution, which of course turned much bloodier. The National Constituent Assembly essentially abolished the old hereditary aristocracy (as well as the church's ability to collect tithes) in its August Decrees of 1789. There remained, however, the awkward problem of what to do with the abolished aristocrats themselves. The Committee on Public Safety, the Jacobin ruling body, decided in the main that the best course, lest the forces of reaction somehow coalesce in and around the ex-nobility, was to chop off their heads.

Americans often like to congratulate themselves on the superiority of the American Revolution to the French Revolution on grounds of the success of the former without recourse to the Terror and such. In doing so, they are seconding the judgment of the eighteenth-century writer and politician Edmund Burke, who supported the American Revolution as an extension of liberty but condemned the French Revolution for its radicalism aimed at the complete overthrow of the institutions of the *ancien régime*, from the monarchy and aristocracy down to the traditional names of the months of the year. Of course Burke had a domestic agenda as well, which was to ensure that England itself under the monarchy remained (or became) "a sanctuary of liberty" for the people. Burke is generally regarded as an iconic conservative political commentator, but here as elsewhere he reveals that the title to which he can best lay claim is that of the first great *liberal* conservative commentator. He was no defender of kings on account of their supposed divine rights, or of aristocrats because of the justice of their hereditary privileges, or of established churches for their ability to coerce their flock into right action by the church's light. Rather, his defense of existing institutions such as the English monarchy derived from his hope, not irrational in the context of England, that the king would be a protector of the liberties of the English people.

As to where the barons and dukes fit into this scheme, they don't: Although in his later work he offered a qualified defense of hereditary aristocracy in the form of the House of Lords, Burke reserved his special praise for a "natural aristocracy" of cultivated individuals—a rather different proposition, and a category into which Burke the Irish commoner himself would readily fit. In fairness, then, and without prejudice to the case against the murderous excesses of the French revolution, one must observe that the Americans had an easier revolution to make precisely because of the absence of an entrenched aristocracy.

In both cases, however, "equality of conditions" in the Tocquevillian sense was on the march, as indeed he perceived it to be elsewhere in Europe at the time, amounting to an irresistible force. This march was something of which Tocqueville generally approved. But he perceived as well that the old aristocratic ways would soon be gone, and he noted unsentimentally that their departure entails a loss. "Equality of conditions," in Tocqueville's view, comes about from a leveling tendency that entails not only a higher status for each individual and his *semblables*, but also cutting the once-higher types down to size—or more precisely, cutting them out of the political and social picture altogether.

Other thinkers have taken a substantially dimmer view of this passion for equality. At the forefront of their ranks was surely Friedrich Nietzsche, who regarded egalitarianism and the democratic sensibility as fundamentally corrosive of great human achievement and the properly more prominent role of the higher type:

> Every enhancement of the type "man" has so far been the work of an aristocratic society—and it will be so again and again—a society that believes in the long ladder of an order of rank and differences of value between man and man, and that needs slavery in one form or other. . . . Let us admit to ourselves, without trying to be considerate, how every higher culture on earth so far has *begun*. Human beings whose nature was still natural, barbarians in every terrible sense of the word, men of prey who were in possession of unbroken strength of will and lust for power, hurled themselves upon weaker, more civilized, more peaceful races. . . . In the beginning, the noble caste was always

the barbarian caste: their predominance did not lie mainly in physical strength but in strength of the soul—they were more *whole* human beings (which also means, at every level, "more whole beasts"). (IX 257)

Aristocracy had its obligations, of course, foremost a readiness and willingness to fight the king's wars when asked. Otherwise, however, the nobles were creatures of leisure: They had no need to work for their daily bread; the labor of their serfs or peasants or vassals served to keep them in comfortable if not high style. They could pass their time as they pleased, perhaps in the cultivation of their own highly stylized code of ethics, from chivalry in the West to *bushido* in medieval Japan. They could commission works of art and patronize the arts or assemble great libraries and collections. And, of course, they would have practiced the art of war from their youngest days, presumably attaining a competence that would serve a king well. There is a certain kind of virtue here—to be precise, aristocratic virtue.

Such virtue entails the cultivation of a sensibility of superiority. One wants "the best" and wishes to be among "the best"—and one has no compunction whatsoever about treating those lower than oneself appropriately, which is to say, as inferiors. As Nietzsche writes:

"Exploitation" does not belong to a corrupt or imperfect and primitive society; it belongs to the *essence* of what lives, as a basic organic function; it is a consequence of the will to power, which is after all the will of life. (IX 259)

Nietzsche contrasts "master morality" with "slave morality." The former is comfortable with high rank and a sense of superiority, sufficient unto itself and confident in its judgment. "The noble type of man experiences *itself* as determining values; it does not need approval; . . . . Noble and courageous human beings . . . are farthest removed from that morality which finds the distinction of morality precisely in pity, or in acting for others. . . ." (IX 260ff). Here, Nietzsche's declaration of war against the egalitarian spirit of the age comes fully to the fore: He has no use for a sensibility grounded in the proposition that others are "like us" unless that "us" stands as a class of masters against a lower class of slaves and the slavish. The master's opinion of himself is self-sufficient; the slave depends on what others think even for a conception of the self.

Yet the older and higher master morality is on the decline. The "slowly arriving democratic order of things" Nietzsche attributes in the first instance to "the intermarriage of masters and slaves" (IX 261) and subsequently to the arrival of conditions of ease and luxury in which maintaining the older and more difficult ways becomes first an option, finally almost an impossibility. The "acute observers and loiterers" from another and better time, such as Nietzsche himself, recognize

> that everything around them is corrupted and corrupts, that nothing will stand the day after tomorrow, except *one* type of man, the incurably mediocre. The mediocre alone have a chance of continuing their type and propagating—they are the men of the future, the only survivors: "Be like them! Become mediocre!" is now the only morality that still makes sense, that still gets a hearing. (IX 262)

Nietzsche's contempt for "equality of conditions" and the emerging sensibility of regard for one's *semblables* could not be clearer.

Somewhat murkier, however, is his description of "master morality" and "aristocratic society" as the wellspring of "the enhancement of the type 'man.'" Nietzsche rose to the defense of aristocracy at the moment it was on the way out. He knew that, of course. But he doesn't really seem to take into consideration that precisely to the extent one considers the aristocracy and its "master morality" a higher human type, one must acknowledge that it is a *lower form* of the higher type. Aristocracy is inferior to the classically heroic king and what one might call, following Machiavelli's lead, "prince morality," the sometimes bloody-minded set of guidelines he offers to a ruler to maintain himself in power. One element of this task is managing other potentially powerful characters who might pose a threat. As we have seen, better to acknowledge that aristocracy itself has its origins in "prince morality," to which aristocracy has its uses—namely, taming (albeit imperfectly) heroic impulses that might threaten the king and the political order he represents.

Nietzsche yearned for a Superman, and one can see in this yearning a desire for the return of a classical hero at a time when such human beings were increasingly rare in the modern world of his day (though not yet completely gone from it). I think it is hardly beyond reason (though, per Nietzsche, it may indeed be "beyond good and evil") to note the incompatibility of the classical hero with politics in an age of equality and end up preferring an age in which a classical hero could flourish and the egalitarian impulse and those who harbor it were absent or beaten into submission. And indeed, there is something, rather than nothing, to admire in the aristocratic virtues, including the willingness to risk one's life in defense of one's honor.

But if it's rank one praises, should one not look all the way to the top of the ladder to bestow the highest praise? And should one not acknowledge that the next few rungs down, with their dukes and barons and knights, though higher than many, are lower than the highest? And should one not be just as interested, as we have been here, in what makes them lower than the highest as in what makes them higher than the low?

Would a great warrior sulk in his tent while his comrades suffered declining fortune in battle? No, *a* great warrior would not. But Achilles, the *greatest* warrior, would. Achilles, by his own light, is in no sense generic. He is not *of a type*. He comports himself in a fashion that suits himself. His virtue, if we want to call it that, is singular. I have spoken loosely here of the classical heroic type, proffering a formal definition with two elements: a) a willingness to risk death as necessary, and b) as a dictate of an inner sense of superiority, greatness or perfection. But as a matter of self-perception, heroes have no peers. To the extent they are given to reflection, their comparison of self to others is likely not to their contemporaries, but to historical figures whose heroic deeds they admire even as they contemplate surpassing them. Thus Alexander's copy of the

*Iliad* under his pillow at night; thus Caesar's disappointment in himself that Alexander conquered the world at an age Caesar had already passed.

Nietzsche's contentions to the contrary notwithstanding, in the case of aristocratic virtue, there is no self-sufficiency in point of view; one's peers are of the essence. Already, "master morality" and "slave morality" are conjoined by the need for contrast. In a given situation, an adherent of "master morality" behaves differently from an adherent of "slave morality," and the aristocratic former have a shared sense of this difference.

The masters perceive other masters as kindred. Their shared morality is not something akin to a revealed religion to which they submit. That would make them slavish. Rather, master morality (or, less tendentiously, aristocratic virtue) is a code of behavior of which they are collective custodians. They are "other-directed." The sense of honor and dishonor is about how one stands in the view of others, a frame of judgment about oneself that stands apart from oneself. It is quite different from the self-sufficiency of a hero in the classical sense.

The "enhancement of the type 'man'" that is the work of aristocracy, in Nietzsche's view, is necessarily a refinement of what is given or lower, the raw material of the human. Yet perhaps surprisingly, "enhancement" has a limit, and the limit is that which one's aristocratic peers deem necessary and sufficient. There is a mutual recognition of equality in superiority, and the barons and knights adhered to it not only by their disdain for low behavior but also by refraining from asserting a personal sense of superiority to their peers and their way of life. Once again, this sets them apart from heroes in the classical sense.

For his sense of "master morality" and "slave morality," Nietzsche drew heavily on the German idealist philosopher G.W.F. Hegel's famous dialectic of the master and the slave (though Nietzsche dismissed Hegel's affinity for the spread of freedom and equality, whose phenomenological origin is in the master-slave dialectic). In Hegel's description, two individuals come into conflict. Each is willing to risk his life in a competition to the death. When two such types meet, only one can survive. But if one of the parties is willing to risk death and the other is not, the result is a relationship of master to slave, as the master grants the slave his life in exchange for the slave's service. Aristocracy is in this sense a society of masters who regard one another as peers. The serfs don't count.

Hegel, like Tocqueville, was writing against the backdrop of an aristocratic society, but one in which he likewise detected the movement of Spirit in the direction of freedom. In that sense, the serfs do count over time, as they cultivate through their work as slaves a certain mastery of their own over nature, and develop among themselves a consciousness of their own resulting freedom, a freedom they acknowledge among themselves through their mutual recognition of each other's freedom. That's the only way the wind blows, and it's the same wind Tocqueville felt blowing gently through the Old World and at gale force in the New.

Yet we are left with the same serious question in Hegel's first resolution of the master-slave dialectic, that of a society of masters alongside a society of slaves. Why don't these aristocratic masters, unafraid of risking their lives, battle it out among each other for final supremacy? Hegel's answer seems to be that they are satisfied with the mutual recognition of equality among themselves. If that's true, however, it's because the spirit of the classical hero has been successfully tamed—trained, that is, to accept this sense of equality among superior peers as sufficient to satisfy whatever remains of the inner sense of greatness beating within the breast.

Hegel regarded aristocratic equality as a temporary resolution of the master-slave dialectic, insofar as it would be subject to challenge from below, as the spirit of freedom developed among the soon-to-be former slaves. But aristocratic equality is likewise subject to challenge the other way, when an aristocrat wishes to assert his superiority over fellow aristocrats by risking death in a contest for supremacy. Historically, this happened not infrequently. The Wars of the Roses are among the more famous of innumerable examples. And in such circumstances, even those quite satisfied with the benefits of noble birth would usually find themselves in a position in which they had to take one side or the other, at considerable personal risk. Picking the wrong side could easily mean death.

But warfare for supremacy didn't happen all the time, or among all aristocrats. The gentry were not typically in a "state of nature" amongst themselves. They generally aimed their sights lower than supreme power. So it is that what looks "higher"—aristocrats and the aristocratic virtues—must also be understood as lower: lower than supreme heroic achievement in the classical sense.

The critique of modernity focused on its leveling effect with regard to the possibility of human achievement has no basis for halting its inquiry with praise for aristocracy and aristocratic virtue (or "master morality"). It ought to recognize aristocratic virtue as a falling away from classically heroic virtue. If the evolution of political power from the rule of "one" to that of "a few" to that of "many" or "all" really describes a rank, which I don't think it does, then the highest is "one." Besides, the instability of aristocratic order was already apparent by the time Nietzsche rose to its defense. How much "higher" than egalitarian political order could aristo-cratic order have been if egalitarian political order was so comprehensively able to undermine and destroy it, if not indeed to chop off its heads?

As noted, we have been maintaining a fairly tight grip on a "formal" understanding of heroism. A hero is someone willing to risk death out of fidelity to an inner sense of greatness. But with Nietzsche's rebellion against "slave morality" and its concern "for others" and sense of "pity," the moment arrives at which we need to add some content to the ques-tion of the heroic, lest we fall into perverse results.

Heroism is bound to some degree to place and identity. From a sufficient historical remove, one can perceive in Achilles and Alexander heroism as such. But those observing either figure contemporaneously would likely find their views influenced by whether they were Greek on the one side, or Trojan or from somewhere in Asia minor on the other. One has a different regard for the conqueror depending on whether one's side is doing the conquering or being conquered.

This has always been true, and it has usually been irrelevant to the broader consideration of heroism. Machiavelli is not wrong that historical judgment is generally kind to the winners and harsh on the losers. If Tokhtaymish had come out on top over Timur and gone on to conquer Central Asia, we would say the same things about Tokhtaymish that we say about Timur, and Timur would be an example of history's losers. There is little to no basis for the expression of a preference for the cause of Timur over that of Tokhtaymish, or vice versa.

There are exceptional cases, to be sure. Machiavelli himself grants as much. In the pursuit of power, there are certain limits to the egregious abuse of other human beings beyond which praise is inappropriate. His principal example is Agathocles of Syracuse, who lived from 361 to 289 BCE:

> [H]e rose through [the military's] ranks to become praetor of Syracuse. . . . [O]ne morning, he assembled the people and Senate of Syracuse as if he had to decide things pertinent to the republic. At a signal he had ordered, he had all the senators and the richest of the people killed by his soldiers. Once they were dead, he seized and held the principate of the city without any civil controversy. . . . Yet one cannot call it virtue to kill one's citizens, betray one's friends, to be without faith, without mercy, without religion; these modes can enable one to acquire empire, but not glory. (VIII)

My tone in describing Crassus's roadside crucifixion spectacle probably conveyed disapproval. Perhaps this would qualify Crassus for a Machiavellian exception to what one can "call . . . virtue" (though perhaps not). Likewise, I hope it's evident that my admiration for Lucretia extends beyond her heroic deed as such to approval for her role in bringing down a corrupt dynasty.

But at some point, substantive moral judgment apart from considerations of whose side you are on seem inevitable. One could debate the theoretical merits of Nietzsche's radical preference for "master morality" over "slave morality." But there isn't really much of a debate over the twentieth-century regime that saw itself presiding over a "master race."

Neutrality on the merits, and an examination merely of Adolph Hitler's willingness to risk his life in pursuit of his ambition and sense of destiny (or, to be perfectly candid, his inner sense of greatness), would be a grotesque exercise in the perversity of abstraction. The same must be said of Osama bin Laden.

Here again, Tocqueville's "equality of conditions [as] the generative fact" of modern times comes to the fore, and with it the sense of others "like us"—not in the sense of "us" versus "them," or one side versus another, but of human affinity that is in principle, if not yet in fact, universal. Hitler's "us," like bin Laden's two generations later, was in principle exclusionary. To the extent their visions were universal, it was not in the sense of voluntary affinity but of conquest and the elimination of the "other."

This, I believe, makes them *villains*. The word conjoins a notion of an adversary with a sense of substantive moral disapproval on the part of the person using it. Its origin in English is *villein*, which refers to a peasant or someone low-born. The sense is "base," and in many instances today, it remains plausible to say that a villain is someone who acts basely. But we must not shackle ourselves to the aristocratic age in which the term was born. The implied rank order of "low" and "high" in that age is something we have been examining critically. It is not "low" but reprehensible to pursue the creation of a Thousand-Year Reich dedicated to the rightful rule of the Aryan race. Likewise, there is nothing "low" but everything reprehensible about beheading all those standing in the way of the restoration of the caliphate.

In the modern world, the recrudescence of the classically heroic type inevitably entails villainy. The willingness to risk one's life in service to an inner ambition or sense of greatness *at war with the "equality of conditions" of the modern age* is nowadays villainy pure and simple.

## CHAPTER 6

# THE BACKLASH AGAINST THE SLAYING HERO

*World War I and the turn against the pursuit of military glory.*
*Twentieth-century revisionism on "great" figures from the past.*
*Birth of the antihero.*

We have been tracing the emergence of a kind of political order that is antithetical to the classical hero. It is egalitarian political order, one in which people look at one another and perceive not a difference of rank but rather persons "like themselves," in Tocqueville's characterization (408). The simplest thing to say is that egalitarian political order has no place for a classical hero and is in fact designed to prevent the emergence of such a character.

I have used the term "designed" not just in the weak sense of a necessary condition for how things have turned out historically: It's true that we have the wide dispersion of democratic political order and the simultaneous disappearance from the scene of the likes of Achilles, Alexander, and Julius Caesar; there is a fundamental incompatibility here. But political order was *designed* in the strong sense as well, designed precisely *by* the upholders of pre-modern political order seeking to protect that order from the destabilizing effects of the arrival of the classically heroic type. The round table of the king was one such method; then came the sovereign's establishment of hereditary feudal privileges more broadly; then, finally, the sometimes bloody elite acts of creation of a kind of political order that would not be prone to the emergence of an abusive aristocracy *or* an abusive king: democratic political order.

But it was not enough merely to, so to speak, banish the classical hero—to make sure that any youngster exhibiting Achillean or Alexandrian tendencies on the playground gets appropriate counseling and if necessary medication to set aside his or her bullying ways before they turn into a desire to rule the world. The present, as we noted briefly in the previous chapter, is also prone to the recrudescence of the past. Historical figures, especially those of the heroic type, outlive their own mortality in the retelling of their deeds of greatness down to the present. For Alexander, Achilles was not only past but prologue. If such tales inspire people of the present age to take up the old heroic ways, the result could potentially be no less dangerous to modern political order than heroes were to the old orders.

So lest it continue to inspire, the way of the conquering hero needs to be discredited. In addition to practical banishment from the playground, there also emerged a democratic revisionist account of the heroic type *tout court*. It had two principal components. The first was the effort to categorize the classically heroic type as a figure of no contemporary significance. Achilles, Alexander, Caesar—these were ineluctably creatures of a distant past. They were under no circumstances figures people could or should emulate in the present. On the contrary, someone professing a sincere desire to conquer the world would be taken not seriously but as a candidate for an insane asylum. Thus the *study* of classical heroism becomes yet another attempt to reduce the danger of the classically heroic type, to cut that type down to size and out of the modern picture, only this time posthumously.

Heroes become contextualized, such that we try to understand Achilles in light of Greek civilization and political order of the eighth century BCE and Alexander in light of that of the fourth century BCE—rather than, say, trying to understand Greek civilization and political order in the eighth or fourth century BCE in light of Achilles and Alexander, as Homer and Plutarch seem to think best. Once we have placed such heroes under glass in this fashion, we are safe from them. Or so we like to think.

The second component of the democratic revisionist account sought to discredit the activity at the heart of most expressions of classical heroism. That activity was killing.

Although we have touched upon it in previous chapters, we haven't really dwelt on this point hitherto, because I have been emphasizing a trait more fundamental to the heroic type, namely, the willingness to risk one's own life. But this willingness was not merely a quality of mind or spirit that rarely had occasion to express itself. On the contrary, the classical hero was a *slaying* hero, a dealer of bloody death to the unfortunates who fell in his or her path. Lucretia, who directly took only her own life, was an exception, but the body counts an Achilles or an Alexander racked up personally—or any lesser hero celebrated locally anywhere at that time and for centuries thereafter—were simply staggering.

Now, the ancient world was not lacking for a sense of the pity of war and the pathos of the dying. We have seen poor, miserable Tros, devoting his last mortal moments to begging Achilles unsuccessfully for his life. So it's not as if it has failed to occur to Homer that "war is hell," in the blunt assessment widely attributed to General William Tecumseh Sherman 25-plus centuries later. Yet clearly Homer is of the view that the slaying hero is worth our attention because a certain kind of greatness does indeed manifest itself in the act of slaughtering one's enemies. Homer did not write the *Iliad* merely to shower Achilles with glory, and for that matter neither did the author of Gilgamesh see the king of Uruk as merely glorious and wholly admirable. Both find the heroes at the center of their respective tales worth examining in some detail and not uncritically—to enlighten nonheroic types (such as ourselves, in most cases) about what makes them tick. Nevertheless, there is no avoiding the conclusion that Homer and other classical authors describing heroic deeds do indeed understand themselves as engaged in the depiction of greatness, of certain human beings superior to almost all others.

In modern times, one might hear the activity of these writers described as the glorification of violence. And indeed, the twentieth century saw a large-scale backlash against heroics in the slaying form.

For most of the past hundred years, the cultural depiction of war has centered on the soldiers doing the fighting. The result has been innumerable intimate portraits of horror, brutality, and violent death designed to engender in the reader or viewer sensations of mortal dread, of hope mixed with desperation, of confusion and uncertainty, supposedly akin to the sensations soldiers feel in the heat of battle.

The soldier's-eye view of war is not the only possible cultural perspective on war, of course. Clearly Shakespeare attaches more importance to what King Henry V had to say to his soldiers at Agincourt that St. Crispian's Day in 1415 than to what the rest of the band of brothers fighting on his side might be thinking on the eve of the battle. Nor does Shakespeare's Henry fail to speak to us to this day.

Yet it is also true that no one alive today is much like Henry—nor Achilles, Alexander, Caesar, Pompey, and the host of others whose exploits were once at the center of reflections on war and peace. Perhaps we don't hear much about warrior-kings and conquerors simply because the modern world doesn't produce that type of character any more. The correlation seems clear cut, but I think that line of argument may reverse the causation: It seems equally plausible that we don't run into that type of character in reality anymore because we no longer attach special status or reverence to conquering, slaying heroes. Just the opposite.

The focus on the soldier's-eye view of war is hardly surprising in a century distinguished by the creation of a mass culture on one hand and the flourishing of individualism on the other. Why wouldn't we be keenly interested in war considered through the prism of the soldier? In a country full of Tocqueville's people "like themselves," citizen-soldiers are people like us as well. Their stories are in some sense our own, or could be. It's not wildly implausible to imagine oneself in the place of those like us. The sympathetic imagination can certainly extend to the fear and exhilaration of mortal combat.

The modern world's imperative to focus on the individual in wartime certainly received an indirect boost during the past century from the human disaster wreaked by war-worshipping regimes and terrorist organizations indifferent to the suffering of others. For them, war and violent death were (and, in the case of al Qaeda and others, still are) the stuff of anonymous spectacle. They take pride in, their indifference to the suffering of the individuals they target, if indeed they do not revel in the slaughter.

Ernst Jünger, a right-wing German intellectual who came to prominence during the interwar years, wrote in a disturbing 1934 treatise *On Pain* (one of many of his works that still disturb) of the arrival of a form of mass society, decoupled from liberal individualism, whose primary purpose is preparation for and engagement in war:

> Today, we can say with some certainty that the world of the self-gratifying and self-critical individual is over and that its system of values, if no doubt still widespread, has been overthrown in all decisive points or refuted by its very own consequences. . . . The heroic worldview is granted to the hero solely by right of birth. . . . The same is true for race altogether; a race exists and is recognized through its actions. A total state . . . presupposes the existence of at least one single total human being. . . . In relation to cultic associations, . . . the advent of a god is independent of human effort. (17–18)

The measure of human beings in such a society or total state is their ability to bear hardship and pain, especially in wartime: "a breed of men resolute in obedience to authority." What might that entail?

> In order to make clear just how high the demands on preparedness have become, consider a practical example. Recently a story circulated in the newspapers about a new torpedo that the Japanese navy is apparently developing. The weapon has an astounding feature. It is no longer guided mechanically but by a human device—to be precise,

by a human being at the helm, who is locked in a tiny compartment and regarded as a technical component of the torpedo a well as its actual intelligence.

. . . To link another thought to the idea of a human projectile, it is obvious that with such a stance man is superior to every imaginable multitude of individuals. (18–19)

Jünger, like a number of his contemporaries on the German right, is both unattractive in the extreme and somewhat slippery. He mostly presents himself as merely describing a new post-liberal world that is coming into being, distancing himself from advocacy on its behalf and uncertain about what is to come. Yet it is impossible to avoid the conclusion that a polemicist is at work here, and that in Jünger's view a "total state" of torpedo-men under the control of a "single total human being" is a set of arrangements superior to anything we might be referring to eighty years later when we use the term "modern world." If fascism of the Nazi variety turned out not to be precisely what Jünger had in mind—he wrote an allegorical novel in 1939 widely understood as critical of the Hitler regime, and had a distinguished intellectual career after the war, dying at age 102 in 1998—nevertheless, the progress of fascism and its quest for a revived sense of the conquering hero/race/superman was certainly abetted by works such as *On Pain.*

It is perhaps ironic that Jünger first came to fame because of his searing memoir of World War I, *Storm of Steel.* The torpedo-man, after all, will leave behind no memoir of his "resolute . . . obedience to authority." Yet the test of arms in World War II resulted in the defeat of fascism at the hands of a coalition of nations whose most powerful member, the United States, most completely exemplified democratic, bourgeois society and its "multitude of individuals." This defeat served powerfully to discredit the glorification of death due to "resolute . . . obedience" and to return attention to the individual.

Conscription also figures into the emerging focus on the individual in wartime. The fact is that whether to face violent death in battle was often the most important choice *denied* an individual in a century of rising individualism. This fact was problematic even in the case of wars that enjoyed broad popular support as necessary and just. When a war became unpopular, the problem could become acute. Although the military historian S.L.A. Marshall's notorious 1947 conclusion that only 3 in 10 infantrymen in World War II actually fired their weapons has now been widely discredited, a more careful 1987 survey by Russell W. Glenn of 258 1st Cavalry Division Vietnam veterans revealed that, indeed, some smaller percentage did not fire their primary weapons, and that in some cases fear was a factor (though not necessarily irrational fear, nor did the fear factor typically exert a constant grip on an individual such that there were no circumstances in which he would fire). In any case, it is certain that some combat situations leave an individual soldier with no good options—and plausible in such cases that the compulsory character of one's participation would be an aggravating factor (though we must be careful not to conclude from this that those who have volunteered will always remain happy warriors at peace with their decision to do so).

In thinking about war, therefore, we have many good reasons for our cultural focus on Everyman in extremis. But let us not forget another fact about this perspective on war: Generally speaking, its propagators have had an agenda. Their ambitions extend far beyond aesthetic realism—blood, body parts, and all. They are also in a general sense antiwar.

They may (or may not) concede the necessity of war or its inevitability; they may (or may not) hold the view that the test of combat can bring out the best in a human being as well as the worst. But assuredly, they see no glory or opportunity for glory in what they portray; to them, no one who has known war could rationally seek war, except (perhaps) in times of dire emergency.

The senseless slaughter of trench warfare in World War I produced a generation of writers who aimed to discredit once and for all the figure of the slaying conqueror-hero and the broader pursuit of battlefield glory. This literature, often written out of the bitter personal experience of a very strange, startlingly cruel, and very long war, portrayed the essence of war as nothing more than individual suffering and death.

The literature of World War I did not begin from this position. A more conventionally romantic view of war and of sacrifice for King and country characterized some of the earliest offerings from poet-soldiers. Such was the case with the extraordinarily talented and beautiful Rupert Brooke. While serving in the Royal Navy, he created a huge stir on the home front, not long before his death from sepsis on the eve of the disastrous Gallipoli landing, with what would become his most famous verses, "V. The Soldier," the fifth in a sequence of sonnets also called "The Soldier." It moved many a stalwart Englishman to tears:

> If I should die, think only this of me,
>> That there's some corner of a foreign field
> That is forever England. There shall be
>> In that rich earth a richer dust concealed;
> A dust whom England bore, shaped, made aware,
>> Gave, once, her flowers to love, her ways to roam,
> A body of England's breathing English air,
>> Washed by the rivers, blest by suns of home.

One can understand why the Dean of St. Paul's Cathedral in London read it aloud to the congregation on Easter Sunday 1915: Could there be a more beautiful way to rally the English people to the cause? But really: the hastily dug graves into which the brutalized bodies of the war dead were placed and covered over were hardly reconstituted as "forever England" thereby.

In a way, Brooke's poem is really a gentler version (though no less sentimental) of the speech Henry V gives (in Shakespeare's telling) on the eve of his great victory over the French at Agincourt:

> We few, we happy few, we band of brothers;
> For he to-day that sheds his blood with me

Shall be my brother; be he ne'er so vile,
This day shall gentle his condition;
And gentlemen in England now-a-bed
Shall think themselves accurs'd they were not here,
And hold their manhoods cheap whiles any speaks
That fought with us upon Saint Crispin's day. (Act IV, scene 3, 60–67)

If you are a king trying to rally soldiers to great exertion, what can it hurt to suggest something manifestly untrue, namely, that thereafter the survivors will be brothers? As in, potential heirs to the throne, you mean? Well, no. Maybe welcome any time to a private bedchamber in the royal castle? No, not that either. But brothers.

Brooke's poetry came to be roundly despised by many of his literary contemporaries for its sentimentality and its unmooredness from the actual experience of war. Consider, by way of contrast, Charles Hamilton Sorley, who died at the age of 20 in 1915 at the battle of Loos. Here is his assessment of the essence of war, from a poem called "Route March":

On marching men, on
To the gates of death with song.
Sow your gladness for earth's reaping,
So you may be glad though sleeping.
Strew your gladness on earth's bed,
So be merry, so be dead.

Or:

When you see millions of the mouthless dead
Across your dreams in pale battalions go,
Say not soft things as other men have said.
Give them not praise. For, deaf, how could they know
It is not curses heaped upon each gashed head?

What we have here is a radical decoupling, a rejection of any transcendent meaning that might accompany death in wartime. The living must recognize that the dead neither know nor care what anyone might say. Accordingly, the notion that one should conduct oneself in a way that wins acclaim or glory after one is gone becomes purest folly, as does the notion that one is fighting or dying *for* something—oneself or one's country.

The British poet Wilfred Owen likewise did not survive the war; he died in action mere days before the Armistice. But as he fought, he too composed a body of work that depicts the horror of war with searing intensity and whose purpose is blatantly polemical. His most famous poem is "Dulce et Decorum Est," whose title comes from a line in one of the Roman poet Horace's *Odes*: "*dulce et decorum est pro patria mori*," or "sweet and fitting it is to die for one's country." Owen describes an attack by poison gas on a group of weary soldiers bound for the rear:

> Gas! Gas! Quick boys!—An ecstacy of fumbling,
> fitting the clumsy helmets just in time,
> But someone still was yelling out and stumbling
> and flound'ring like a man in fire or lime . . .
> ***
> If in some smothering dreams you too could pace
> Behind the wagon that we flung him in,
> And watch the white eyes writhing in his face,
> His hanging face, like a devil's sick of sin,
> If you could hear, at every jolt, the blood
> Come gargling from the froth-corrupted lungs
> ***
> My friend, you would not tell with such high zest
> To children ardent for some desperate glory,
> The old lie, *Dulce et decorum est*
> *Pro patria mori.*

I don't really know what the face of a devil "sick of sin" would look like, and I have omitted at the second ellipsis two lines that create a net loss in the literary merit of the poem. But never mind literary merit; considered as a polemic, the poem is truly excellent. It sets up Horace as a kind of monster, an old man who knows better, or should, but is content to propagandize impressionable youth into marching cheerfully off to their doom. Whatever the merits of fighting—for one's country or for one's own ambition—there is nothing about violent death that is sweet or fitting to the dead, since (per Sorley) they are simply dead; nor in most cases is one's last perception in the act of dying in war likely to be a sense of the sweet fitness of one's death—except perhaps in a rueful sense, if one is of the sort able even in extremis to cultivate irony.

As for those giving the orders, we can turn to Siegfried Sassoon, who fought throughout the war, for an assessment of the senior military leadership's view of the soldiers they were sending into battle. Here is his short poem "The General," whose backdrop is the April–May 1917 battle of Arras, a bloody and unsuccessful British attempt to break through the German lines:

'Good morning, good morning!' the General said
When we met him last week on our way to the line.
Now the soldiers he smiled at are most of 'em dead
And we're cursing his staff for incompetent swine.

'He's a cheery old card,' grunted Harry to Jack
As they slogged up to Arras with rifle and pack.
      *       *       *
But he did for them both by his plan of attack.

As for the home front, the celebration of supposed heroics with ticker-tape parades was nothing more than the way in which the politically powerful, acting out of their own cynical self-interest, persuaded young people to serve as cannon fodder. Sassoon again, in "'They'":

The Bishop tells us, 'When the boys come back,
They will not be the same, for they'll have fought
In a just cause; they lead the last attack
On Anti-Christ; their comrade's blood has bought
New right to breed an honorable race.
They have challenged Death and dared him face to face.'


'We're none of us the same,' the boys reply.
'For George lost both his legs; and Bill's stone blind;
Poor Jim's shot through the lungs and like to die;
And Bert's gone syphilitic; you'll not find
A chap who's served who hasn't found some change.'
And the bishop said: 'The ways of God are strange.'


The mortal enemy of the poets here is abstraction: any effort to make war about something other than what happens to George and Bill and Jim (though it seems undeniably an abstraction, albeit of a different kind, to pin Bert's syphilis on the war). Those who talk about war in abstract terms, whether as a matter of strategic necessity or national interest or moral imperative or God's will being done, are engaged in the willful act of making war easier by turning our attention away from George and Bill. Even a general saying "good morning" is perpetrating a lie, smug in his safety somewhere other than "the line."

What began as a mostly British literary phenomenon, this vivid and personal perspective on war, got a distinctly American voice with the cultural response to the morass of Vietnam. The antiwar, antiheroic, antiglorious embrace of the perspective of the combat soldier was the animating characteristic of most of the media coverage of Vietnam as the war wore on. *Newsweek*, for example, in the section of the magazine devoted each week to "The War in Vietnam," often published accounts like this one (from November 1, 1965):

From the shore, the guerrillas cut loose with a torrent of heavy-weapons and small-arms fire that churned up the water around the patrol. The fourth boat in line rocked drunkenly as three recoilless rifle rounds tore into it. Its captain, bleeding from shrapnel wounds, yelled into his radio, "Help me, help me. All of us are wounded or killed and we are sinking." As he spoke, the boat swung out of control and ran aground.

*Life* magazine occupied a position at the apex of American photo-journalism when photojournalism itself was at its peak, at a time just before the advent of video images of war (whether documentary or hyperrealistically contrived fiction). Its pages offered perhaps the most intimate perspective on soldiers at war and victims of war then available. Its photographs from the war were in many instances unforgettable, and the texts that accompanied them were evidently intended to rival them in intimacy. I have a vivid recollection, from age 11, of one of its covers. It was the issue dated January 21, 1972. On a black background lay an official army portrait of a smiling young man. The cover text read: "The One Boy Who Died—A Week's Dead in Vietnam—SP4 Jerry N. Duffey, 1951–1971, Charlotte, Michigan." Inside, the story included an account of his death:

> Thirty minutes after midnight on Dec. 12—at 11:30 A.M., Dec. 11 in Charlotte, Michigan—Acting Sergeant Jerry N. Duffey pulled on his clothes, laced up his jungle boots and took his place as guard sergeant for the shift they call "the graveyard watch" on Hill 131. It was a moonless night, especially dark without the perimeter lights. Thirty-three minutes later, while Jerry was in a hootch, a devastating mortar barrage pounded the lonely garrison. Twenty VC sappers slipped through the jagged wire and systematically blew up buildings with their satchel charges. It was over in twenty minutes. The hilltop was ablaze. Nine of the 17 GI's were injured and Jerry Duffey was dead—three days before he was to go home for Christmas and, as it

turned out, just nineteen days before Hill 131 was to be turned over to the South Vietnamese.

This style, bringing the reader into the combat zone to see the violence and destruction of the war, was also popular in more prestigious journals like the *New Yorker*, which in 1967 published Jonathan Schell's "The Village of Ben Suc," a graphic chronicle of the efforts of United States and South Vietnamese forces to drive the Vietcong from a village on the Saigon River, the conclusion of which describes two American soldiers' forced rationalization of their decision to open fire and kill a young man on a bicycle. (The intimate perspective on war is not always sympathetic to the soldiers.) And in Vietnam, for the first time, camera crews were on hand to cover the war as its major events and battles occurred. They enjoyed remarkably easy and uncensored access to the combat zones, and the footage subsequently broadcast showed soldiers in action as they had never been seen before. The cameras brought the audience into the middle of firefights, artillery barrages, napalm attacks, and helicopter assaults; in the aftermath, the cameras might linger both on the material wreckage and on the dead.

Vietnam was the journalists' war par excellence. But like previous wars, Vietnam also produced a number of veterans with literary ambitions. C.D.B. Bryan, the author of *Friendly Fire*, a nonfiction account of a young soldier killed in Vietnam by American shelling, has described the typical Vietnam narrative in these terms:

> A young white male . . . enlists in the army. . . . He arrives [in Vietnam] nervous, excited, eager, wanting to do good, to *be* good, feeling he is fulfilling part of his destiny, and within forty-eight hours he is sent to a combat unit to replace a kid who didn't last long enough for anyone to learn his name. The kid made a mistake, our young man is told, the kind of mistake that gets people killed. . . . Before the end, of course, there is the first patrol, which our young man goes out on as though he were going to a movie until all hell breaks loose and suddenly he

is in the movie and it is more real than anything he has ever experienced. . . . There is the atrocity scene, to demonstrate that My Lai was not an isolated incident. . . . There are helicopter assaults into hot LZ's [landing zones] . . . and then there are the battle scenes. . . . The Generic Vietnam War Narrative charts the gradual deterioration of order, the disintegration of idealism, the breakdown of character, the alienation from those at home, and, finally, the loss of all sensibility save the will to survive.

Bryan means no disrespect in offering his generic description; indeed, he professes a high regard for several Vietnam *romans à clef*—he names *Fields of Fire* by James Webb, *The 13th Valley* by John Del Vecchio, *A Rumor of War* by Philip Caputo, and *Fragments* by Jack Fuller. But his generic account is an accurate one. What we have in the narratives he discusses are soldiers in combat, and alone; absent from consideration are officers in charge of operations at a level higher than that of the platoon, to say nothing of strategists or politicians. And the Vietnam novels and memoirs are indeed generally preoccupied with the "deterioration" and "disintegration" of the soldier to the exclusion of all else—the anti-glorious reality of fighting.

As with novels, so with memoirs. A helicopter pilot named Robert Mason published one called *Chickenhawk*, a best-selling account of his experience flying soldiers into and out of patrol areas. He too makes the case for understanding the war from the soldier's point of view:

> The local war, the one I was in, went on every day. I was part of it. In the air, I did my job the best I knew how. I flew, as did all pilots, into hot LZ's, because in the middle of the confusion the hazy principles over which the war was fought disappeared. Everything else was excluded. (430)

Near the end of his time in Vietnam, Mason reports, he began to have nightmares, which continued when he returned to the United

States. His deterioration eventually caused him to be grounded from flying helicopters, and he quit the army. The last two paragraphs of the book inform us that he was convicted of trying to smuggle marijuana into the United States, and was free pending appeal. That the war was psychologically devastating to him is irrefutable: he himself bears witness.

The Vietnam War also produced oral histories in large numbers. In 1983, *Newsweek* reunited the surviving members of a company of soldiers who were in Vietnam from 1968 to 1969. The magazine devoted a long cover story to their reunion, including lengthy accounts of the soldiers' recollection of the war; the article was subsequently expanded and published as *Charlie Company: What Vietnam Did to Us*. An acclaimed book by journalist Myra MacPherson, *Long Time Passing: Vietnam and the Haunted Generation*, recorded at some length the thoughts and recollections both of those who fought in the war and of those who opposed it in America. The book means to explore the lasting trauma of the experience of the war. Quoting Studs Terkel, MacPherson refers to those she has interviewed as "my 'improvised battalion of survivors'" (7).

In *Bloods*, the journalist Wallace Terry offered the experience of the Vietnam War as told by a dozen black soldiers. Carol Mithers, writing in the *Village Voice* a dozen years after the end of the war, charged a sexist America with forgetting that 10,000 of the Americans who served in Vietnam were women, mostly nurses; she interviewed several, recording their impressions of gruesome scenes at the army hospitals and describing the lasting traumatic effects the experiences had on them.

Yet for all the depiction of war at its most intimately horrific, from the World War I poets through the Vietnam journalists, memoirists, and novelists—and beyond—it seems to me that the most profound politico-cultural expression of this intimate focus on the soldier in combat as the antiheroic, antiglorious, antiwar essence of war is the great work of art that is the Vietnam Veterans Memorial Wall on the Mall in Washington, DC.

Dedicated on Veterans Day 1982, the iconic monument consists of two highly polished triangular black granite walls, their bases set at right angles in a shallow depression in the earth. The upper sides of the two triangles are even with the level of the ground. The lower sides, ten feet and three inches deep where the triangles join, descend from ground level at the vertices some 246 feet to the base. On the two sides are carved the names of the 58,000 Americans who died in the war, arranged according to chronological order of death from the first such in 1959.

The Wall has two inscriptions in addition to the names of the dead. The first is at the apex of the left side of the monument as you face it:

IN HONOR OF THE MEN AND WOMEN OF THE ARMED FORCES OF THE UNITED STATES WHO SERVED IN THE VIETNAM WAR. THE NAMES OF THOSE WHO GAVE THEIR LIVES AND OF THOSE WHO REMAIN MISSING ARE INSCRIBED IN THE ORDER THEY WERE TAKEN FROM US.

The second is at the bottom of the right triangle where the two join at the center of the monument:

OUR NATION HONORS THE COURAGE, SACRIFICE AND DEVOTION TO DUTY AND COUNTRY OF ITS VIETNAM VETERANS. THIS MEMORIAL WAS BUILT WITH PRI- VATE CONTRIBUTIONS FROM THE AMERICAN PEOPLE. NOVEMBER 11, 1982

Now one could say that the monument's reference to "courage, sacrifice and devotion to duty and country" amounts to an attempt to make something larger of the brute fact that 58,000 Americans died in the war. But the inscriptions vanish into insignificance next to the weight of the names on the Wall and the experience of visiting the monument.

Starting at the apex at ground level and walking downward the length of the wall, one begins what one does not initially realize is a gradual descent into a kind of netherworld. At some point on the way, depending on your height, you have descended below ground level. There, you first fully encounter the immensity of the Wall, and the polished gabbro reveals its secret: your own reflection and the reflection of other visitors in the Wall's stone.

The first time I experienced the effect (not long after the Memorial's dedication), I thought the reflections of the visitors in the highly polished surface were a by-product and an aesthetic mistake, a distraction from the names on the Wall and therefore the central commemorative purpose of the memorial. I was wrong.

The point is that the mirror images of the living visitors dwell in the house of the dead—seemingly transported to a cordon behind the implacable plane of the names, the letters of which were not polished after being carved and do not reflect much light. The names of the dead separate the visitors from the images of themselves, an unbridgeable chasm. If people have come to find a particular name, they almost invariably reach out to touch it. In doing so, they come as close to their own reflections in the house of the dead as possible. But the reflections remain trapped. It's a remarkably effective invitation—indeed, a command—to contemplate mortality.

By the time one reaches the bottom, the Wall towers imposingly over even the tallest of visitors, and the desire to escape the realm of the dead can become palpable. The ascent through eye level and then back to grade comes as a relief, but the names don't stop and the self-consciousness of one's reflection in the Wall is ineradicable down to the visibility of merely the toe of one's shoes near the apex at the other end.

The guidelines of the competition that led to the eventual selection of then-20-year-old Maya Ying Lin's stunning design specified a fundamental requirement: that all proposals include the names of each of the 58,000 who died in the war. This is exactly the difference between the Vietnam memorial and the other great national war memorials. The Iwo Jima Monument, sculpted from a famous World War II photograph, depicts five anonymous soldiers determined to raise the American flag in the heat of battle. They are notable not for individual achievement but for their unified pursuit of their purpose, raising the flag. The Tomb of the Unknowns at Arlington Cemetery is explicitly a testament to anonymity, those who fought and died but whose remains could never be identified. The World War II Memorial is purely neoclassical in form and content, on one-half of its oval structure the stone-carved names of great battles from the Pacific Theater and on the other those from the Atlantic. On a daily basis since its opening, the diminishing cadre of veterans of the war as well as their relatives have left behind personal mementoes, which the government collects every day and stores in anonymous warehouses, to what eventual purpose God knows. Maybe the point is that there need be no additional purpose.

The 58,000 names of the Vietnam Veterans Memorial say something completely different: these are the names of the *individuals* who died. They are what matter.

Well before the end of this century, no one will have a living memory of any of these individuals, and not long after that, their lives will be matters of chiefly genealogical interest to distant relatives. I once heard a clergyman remark from the pulpit, *Fifty years after I am dead, no one will know I was ever alive.* One might quibble about the precise span of time, but here was a sobering reminder that a lifetime is short no matter how long. As for those who seek glory to be remembered forever, I wonder how that will work once our sun burns itself out. "Dust thou art, and to dust shalt thou return," as the priests say on Ash Wednesday.

The Vietnam Veterans Memorial was conceived and executed as the twentieth-century backlash against heroism in its classical, slaying form reached its apogee in the modern world, a point from which it has not really descended: unglorious war as, mainly, the death of the dead.

Notwithstanding the resonance of the critique of abstraction in discussion of war, I am not prepared to give the last word in this quarrel to the camp advocating for the "mouthless dead" over the camp that lays principal emphasis on a "band of brothers." The "mouthless dead" poets have a serious hurdle to get over, which is to answer the question of what if anything the point of life is beyond its continuation. In this scenario, one would be a fool to put one's life at risk in the pursuit of glory, because the pursuit of glory in war is folly. One may be coerced into risking and even giving up one's life, but this is always tragic. Why one might *choose* to risk one's life, in war or any other endeavor, is a mystery. The classical hero is gone and nothing replaces the type. Death holds us all equally in sway, and there is no gain to be had from an assertion of mastery over death through the willingness to risk one's life.

But is that all there is? There is no denying that many young people going off to war, from time immemorial down to the present, have done so in possession of the belief that they are fighting for their country. Nor is this obviously a false belief, even if Rupert Brooke's abstract sentimentality is admirable mainly for its beautiful expression. In some individuals, this conviction has accompanied classically heroic deeds, as we will see when we look at some of the winners of the Congressional Medal of Honor, the highest American combat decoration, in Chapter 8.

Moreover, there comes a point at which the aversion to abstraction about war becomes itself a kind of abstraction. The names on the Wall are those of real people, each of whom died young in war. To the extent that one has any concern at all for one's fellow citizens, or for youth, every one of their stories has an ineffable element of sadness. Yet the names on the Wall have a separate physical reality as "the names on the Wall." This corporeality has nothing to do with the stories of the human beings who bore the names. It's about a way of looking at war.

And in the interest of candor, it's simply not the way all soldiers look at war. In fact, the vivid and personal perspective on war yields no fixed view of what war means to the people fighting. This perspective was the one that those most passionately committed to the traduction of military glory adopted in their polemical endeavors. One could fairly say that they expropriated the perspective from authors and artists of the sort once inclined to admire the classical, slaying hero at work—and did so, moreover, with the *intention* of precluding its reappropriation by anyone inclined to such admiration. But one cannot fairly say that they succeeded in linking the vivid and personal perspective inexorably with an antiwar, antiglory, antiheroic stance.

To appreciate both the independence of the soldier's-eye view of war from a polemically antiwar stance and the variety of sentiments on display among those fighting in wartime, one can do no better than Mark Bowden's 1999 bestseller, *Black Hawk Down*, an account of a 1993 firefight in Mogadishu, Somalia, that left 18 Americans dead and dozens more badly wounded. Painstakingly reconstructed after the fact from hundreds of interviews with participants and military records extracted from an initially reluctant Pentagon, the book is certainly an intimate portrait of a horrific battle, pathos of war and all. What is different here is that Bowden has no discernible agenda. Instead, he lets the events and characters speak for themselves.

It's a complicated story, one that richly illustrates the meaning of the phrase, "the fog of war." A task force of Army Rangers and Delta Force operators embarked on a daylight raid in the heart of lawless Mogadishu for the purpose of capturing senior lieutenants to a local warlord. The task force expected to be in and out in less than an hour. But things began to go wrong: An inexperienced Ranger missed the rope on his way out of a helicopter hovering at 70 feet. He needed to be evacuated. A convoy of trucks and Humvees missed turns on the maddeningly complex, unmarked street grid of the wrecked city. As a result of the delay, the Somali resistance mounted. Lucky shots from grenade launchers felled first one Black Hawk helicopter, then another, setting the force to the tortuous, dangerous task of attempting to rescue survivors and retrieve the bodies of the dead. As darkness fell, the task force found itself fragmented, hunkered down, and desperately in need of reinforcement.

Bowden's characters are not literary spokesmen for a point of view on war; neither is the Mogadishu he describes some sort of metaphor for human malevolence; nor is his intercutting between the men on the ground and their commanders out of harm's way an occasion for infusion of irony and other literary artifice. This is the story of the real participants in a very harrowing gunfight at a particular time in a particular place.

As such, the book was positively subversive of the dominant cultural portrait of war during the twentieth century. Yes, there is bloody mayhem here, and the entirely rational fear soldiers feel as they try to withstand a surprisingly furious assault, and the sense of dread and uncertainty gradually mounting with each bit of bad news, and the urgent effort to keep the wounded alive, and the weight of the sudden death of comrades. But that is hardly the whole story. The emotional range here includes pride, righteous anger, a sense of honor, determination, respect, fraternal love, and, in many instances, a richly mordant sense of humor.

These were elite American soldiers. Most were Rangers, meaning they not only enlisted in the army but also volunteered for advanced airborne training and endured the rigors of Ranger school. Others were members of the supersecret Delta Force, masters of the heights of American soldiering. The Rangers and the "D-boys," as the Rangers call them, trained for war every day, practicing to perfection the art and craft of controlled but hellish violence.

More to the point, they wanted to fight. In the nonfiction environment of *Black Hawk Down*, by contrast with much of our culture's intimate portraiture of war, this desire of theirs is no literary contrivance designed to be shattered by exposure to war's horror. Some of them couldn't imagine pursuing another line of work. Some of them looked back on this brutal night in Mogadishu as time well spent and would, of course, do it again.

The feeling was not unanimous, nor for that matter unmixed. Bowden relates some thoughts of Sgt. Mike Goodale during the fight:

> He thought about how much he wanted to go to war, to see combat, and then he thought about all those great war movies and documentaries he'd seen about battles. He knew he'd never see another of those films and feel the same way about it. People really get killed. He found the best way to accept his predicament was to just assume he was dead already. He was dead already. He just kept on doing his job. (255)

But consider also:

[Spec. Shawn] Nelson surveyed the carnage around him and felt wildly, implausibly lucky. How could he not have been hit? It was hard to describe how he felt . . . it was like an epiphany. Close to death, he had never felt so completely alive.... He felt he would never be the same. He had always known he would die someday, the way anybody knows that they will die, but now its truth had branded him. And it wasn't a frightening or morbid thing. It felt more like a comfort. It made him feel more alive. (249–250)

Spec. Chris Schleif is less introspective as he prepares to join a convoy to relieve those still trapped in the city:

The [M-60] gun and ammo can were still slick with [Sgt. Dominick] Pilla's blood and brain matter. Schleif ditched his own weapon and boarded the Humvee with Pilla's. "He didn't get a chance to kill anybody with it," Schleif explained to Specialist Brad Thomas, who like Schleif was heading back out into the city for the third time. "I'm going to do it for him." (268–269)

And we meet Pvt. George Siegler desperately running to leap onto an armored personnel carrier to take him out of the city after that long night:

[He] sprinted up to the hatch . . . just as a voice yelled from inside, "We can only take one more!" [Lt. Larry] Perino already had one leg in the hatch. Out of the corner of his eye Perino saw the younger man's desperation. He withdrew his leg from the hatch and said, cloaking his kindness with officerly impatience, "Come on, Private, come on." It would have been easy for the lieutenant to say he hadn't seen him. Siegler was so moved by the gesture he decided then and there to reenlist. (293)

It is impossible to read *Black Hawk Down* and conclude that this range of emotion, including an appetite for battle even after having had the experience, was anything but real in these men.

The paradox of the intimate portraiture of war is that in the name of preventing the infliction of carnage, it dehumanizes those who fight, transforming them into automatons and victims to make a point. *Black Hawk Down*, by contrast, is truly intimate; the closer we look, the more unmistakable the humanity. But neither are the soldiers here the product of times different from our own. They have their motives for serving in the military, and they seem to have few misgivings in principle about the act of slaying one's enemies. But none of them seems especially motivated by a desire for glory and acclaim. And none of them seems to harbor any impulse to rise directly from captain of the guard to ruler or tyrant or king. They are men of our times, not some other.


The effort to discredit the slaying hero and the pursuit of glory in battle was, in a way, a lesser included case in a broader effort under way contemporaneously to call into question all claims of greatness or exceptional achievement made on behalf of rare individuals. As the claim to superiority of the classical hero was unacceptable in modern times, so too did the modern, egalitarian world revisit the "great man" of historical inquiries past with newfound suspicion.

A revisionist historical literature emerged portraying the heroes of yore not in the old-fashioned celebratory or hagiographic manner, as figures to be emulated, but rather as deeply flawed human beings. Tocqueville might have called it activist leveling: taking the high and mighty down a peg or two on a retail basis.

Near the end of his life, Thomas Jefferson declared that he wished to be known to history as author of the Declaration of Independence and of the Virginia Statute for Religious Freedom and as founder of the University of Virginia. Interestingly, he did not mention "third president of the United States." But neither did he mention "lifelong slave-owner," nor his sexual relationship with one of his slaves, Sally Hemings. To the revisionist historians, the former stood in ironic contrast to the author of the Declaration's proclamation that "all men are created equal." As for Hemings, what could be a greater abuse of a position of power than the exaction of sexual favors from one's slave?

Jefferson was hardly alone among heroes reconstituted warts and all in this antiheroic cultural environment. Winston Churchill's effort to rally a beleaguered country in an existential battle against Nazi Germany probably reckons on the plus side, but must also be understood against the backdrop of his racism and support for colonialism, including British brutality in Kenya. Abraham Lincoln signed the Emancipation Proclamation and saved the Union, but more important, he may also have been confused about his sexual identity.

The problem is that these exercises in leveling leave us at some risk of concluding that *no* deed can be especially heroic and *no* achievement especially great.

Perhaps the ultimate exercise in the zeroing-out of heroism and individual greatness was the radical social determinist position, associated most closely with Marxism but abandoned now and deemed extreme by most Marxists themselves, that the individual simply doesn't matter to the progress of history. Vastly greater forces dictate the course of events: the emergence of capitalism out of feudal order, the alienation of the worker from the means of production, the development of a capitalist class, a bourgeoisie, and a proletariat. Finally, as the class struggle continued to unfold, the Revolution, the dictatorship of the proletariat, collective ownership of the means of production, and the withering away of the state. For some Marxist theorists, the progress of history had nothing to do with the choices of any individual, nor would it into the future.

During World War II, the philosopher and social critic Sidney Hook wrote a book called *The Hero in History* whose project was to refute the social determinist view by demonstrating the importance of individuals in shaping events. His prime example (the irony was intentional) was V. I. Lenin: Hook shows convincingly that in the absence of Lenin's personal leadership and the decisions he made, there would have been no October Revolution in Russia (184–228).

A much attenuated form of the view that the individual matters not at all is the view that most of what an individual does is never properly the subject of praise or blame—because behavior is much less the product of individual initiative than of genetic and environmental influences. Often, this point of view travels under a banner of compassion or empathy: "There, but for the grace of God, goes John Bradford," said the sixteenth-century clergyman John Bradford on seeing condemned men en route to the gallows. The compassionate perspective sits fairly easily with modern egalitarianism. And it is no more false than the opposite perspective, namely, that those who succeed do so solely by dint of hard work and personal strength—that the privileges and disadvantages with which one begins life and grows up have nothing to do with the kind of person who emerges from youth.

To the extent the compassionate perspective fosters regard for others and a sense of obligation toward those less advantaged, it is certainly valuable. But it does not offer especially good guidance on how to live one's own life. Few are those whose circumstances are such that their personal choices account for nothing. Luck is a factor for good or for ill or for both. But it is typically not the only factor that determines life outcomes. Potentially, at least, an unbalanced perspective of compassion can be corrosive, not least among young people thinking about how they will try to live their lives. If they come to believe that making something of themselves is entirely beyond their power, their personal prophecy may end up self-fulfilling. Worse, they may be highly vulnerable to social and cultural signals emphasizing the powerlessness of the individual and the overriding weight of social forces in how people's lives turn out. The result might be unnecessary paralysis, alienation, even rage.

By the mid-twentieth century, the literary figure of the "antihero" came upon the scene—a "rebel without a cause," but with at least the clarity to see through the self-serving pretensions of the powerful. James Dean starred in the movie that defined teen angst for at least two generations, and his tragic death in an automobile accident at the age of 24 had the effect of freezing him in time as the embodiment of the antihero. Holden Caulfield in *The Catcher in the Rye* is as unheroic a protagonist as one will meet; his chief virtue is his ability to recognize the phoniness of others.

By the end of the twentieth century in the modern world, the slaying, conquering hero was a relic of another time, a figure whose exploits would warrant opprobrium if not derision in the unlikely event one should turn up. Osama bin Laden was a figure of great evil to most Americans. We must also frankly acknowledge that he was a hero to many Salafist Muslims, whose break with the decadence of the modern world has rekindled the conquering and slaying passions of the ancient world—a subject to which we will return in the last chapter.

How fascinatingly subversive of both views was the screaming headline (it's called the "wood") on the front page of the *New York Post* the day after the revelation that the Navy SEAL team that killed bin Laden found a cache of pornographic DVDs in his compound in Abbottabad, Pakistan:

OSAMA
BIN
WANKIN'

Now, *that* is cutting someone down to size.

## CHAPTER 7

# VESTIGIAL AND VIRTUAL HEROES

*Redefinitions. Heroism without risk.*
*The hero as entertainer. Partisans and truth-tellers.*
*From mass culture to wikiculture.*

In the mid-nineteenth century, the Scottish man of letters Thomas Carlyle coined the term "Hero-worship," by which he meant the high regard, entirely proper in his view, that ordinary people have had for the great figures of their history. His project in *Lectures on Heroes, Hero-Worship, and the Heroic in History* was to restore greatness to dignity in an age he believed had come to belittle the very possibility of exceptional human achievement. Carlyle claimed, on the contrary,

> Universal History, the history of what man has accomplished in this world, is at bottom the History of the Great Men who have worked here.... All things that we see standing accomplished in the world are properly the outer material result, the practical realization and embodiment, of Thoughts that dwelt in the Great Men sent into the world. (4)

Each of the *Lectures* takes up one of the "six classes of heroes" Carlyle identifies: the hero as divinity, prophet, poet, priest, man of letters, and king. He suggests that the times in which one lives have some bearing on the type of hero who steps forward: the hero-divinity seems to be a figure belonging to the pagan past and is unlikely to resurface. The greatness of the heroic type will always express itself, but it manifests itself in a form appropriate to its times. One age's prophet is another age's playwright is another's king. A young person destined for greatness will find a proper avenue for its expression and travel down it. What distinguished Muhammad *and* Samuel Johnson from their respective contemporaries was greatness or heroism. What distinguished them from *each other* was that the seventh century was ripe for a prophet, the eighteenth for a literary lion.

Nevertheless, Carlyle argues vehemently against the proposition that the times make the man. He asks: What about the numerous manifest historical instances in which a people were in desperate need of a hero and didn't get one—to their ruin? Heroes appear on their own schedule.

This is certainly true of the slaying hero of the classical age. And it is likewise true that the circumstances from which a poet or literary figure emerges are not entirely predictable, nor are they determinative in the sense that some hypothetical proper alignment of nature and conditions of nurture must inevitably yield a prodigious talent. Carlyle's focus on the individuality of the talent that falls within his "six classes" is surely correct.

And yet: Was there ever an instance in which a people, to their ruin, needed a poet or an artist who didn't come? When the Melians voiced the mistaken view that Sparta would come to their assistance in their imminent fight with Athens, it was not a Spartan poet or aulist they were hoping for, but a hero of the Athenian-slaying kind. There is one and only one type of hero who can take on the task of slaying your enemies: a warrior in the mode of the classical hero. A man of letters or a man of the cloth won't do. Yet the slaying hero figures only subsidiarily in Carlyle's typology. And this is true, it seems to me, because Carlyle's objective is not simply to *revive* appreciation for "Great Men" but to broaden the qualifications for heroic greatness. He must do so, in the first instance, to ensure that the possibility of heroism doesn't belong solely to the distant past. If a hero in the mold of Achilles or Julius Caesar is the only type that passes muster, then the near-extinction of this sort by the mid-nineteenth century, let alone the twenty-first, would make heroism a dead letter. So it is that the times in which one lives influence the course of the hero's heroism.

But the times can point a budding hero in more than one direction. I doubt that Carlyle would deny Aristotle status among the "Great Men" on the grounds that Aristotle never conquered the world, as did his pupil Alexander. But Aristotle's philosophical works still reward study today. The question, moreover, of whether the king is superior to the philosopher, or vice-versa, is one for the ages. Greatness, in Carlyle's plausible view, is manifold. In truth, however, and contrary to Carlyle's contention about the decisive influence of one's times per se on the type of hero who emerges, the expression of greatness in one of the manifold possibilities Carlyle explores in his "six classes" seems to have more to do with the sensibility of the great figure in question than the determinative influence of the times—except that the times do seem increasingly to rule out what was once the dominant figure of the heroic sort, namely the slaying hero.

What Carlyle is up to, then, is an attempt to set a new standard for heroism, one decoupled from the slaying and conquering proclivities of the heroes of the classical age. The new heroism must take many forms because, if heroism is confined to its classical form, *there are no more heroes*. The life-risking type has become largely tame in the Europe of the nineteenth century, a laborer on behalf of sovereign power whose reward for good behavior is a strip of cloth called a medal, perhaps accompanied by the acclaim of the multitude and the riches such acclaim can bring.

Carlyle professed himself to be certain of the ultimate success of his project to rehabilitate greatness, veneration of which he considered innate to humankind. He refers to the "indestructibility of Hero-worship":

> We all love great men; love, venerate, and bow down submissive before great men: nay can we honestly bow down to anything else? Ah, does

not every true man feel that he is himself made higher by doing reverence to what is really above him? . . . And to me it is very cheering to consider that no sceptical logic, or general triviality, insincerity and aridity of any Time and its influences can destroy this noble inborn loyalty and worship that is in man. In times of unbelief, which soon have to become times of revolution, much down-rushing, sorrowful decay and ruin is visible to everybody. For myself in these days, I seem to see in this indestructibility of Hero-worship the everlasting adamant lower than which the confused wreck of revolutionary things cannot fall. (12)

Carlyle was a romantic; he was not a systematic thinker, and in keeping with both his romanticism and his theme, praise for hero worship, he had a tendency to gush. But he had genuine hold of a serious problem, namely, the modern world's egalitarian distrust of claims of greatness and heroism. And his purpose was to vindicate regard for high achievement, which he connects to the classical heroes by enlarging the term "hero" to cover all sorts of major endeavor.

Carlyle was aligning himself against what he saw as the leveling tendencies of his times. Yet he was hardly antimodern. There is certainly a large helping of Enlightenment modernity in his proposition that the figure "we all" properly "love, venerate, and bow down submissive before" is not God or the king, but a certain type of human being.

Yet Carlyle clearly has a foot in both the piety of the ancient world and the humanism of the modern. He wants to retain the qualities of reverence ("love, venerate, and bow down") chiefly associated with belief in God, and secondarily with the affect of submission due in the presence of the supremely powerful of this world. But he seeks to abstract these qualities into a generic "Hero-worship" characteristic of all times and places, and due not only to figures of supreme power but also (at times) to poets and priests. He does so in an effort to counter the ascendant "sceptical logic," "unbelief," and decadent "revolution" swirling all around him. He wants to save the modern world from egalitarian excess, to keep a place in it for due regard for greatness, or the heroic. Clearly, he refers to "every *true* man" (emphasis added) feeling himself "made higher by doing reverence to what is really above him" to evade the manifest fact that many of his contemporaries and ours, in the egalitarian spirit of the age, flatly rejected the proposition that there was or is anyone (or anything) "above" them before whom they should "bow down submissive."

Notwithstanding the bravado of its author, Carlyle's project was, on its own terms, a failure. He sought refuge in his abstract coinage "Hero-worship" and his redefinition of the heroic at the historical moment when "bow[ing] down submissive" was finished. An indication of the extent to which the man was overmatched by his times comes in ironic form from the resilience of his term "Hero-worship," which remains common in discourse nearly 200 years later. Carlyle wrote in praise of "Hero-worship." Today, hero worship is something parents tell children, teachers tell students, and friends admonish each other not to engage in.

Perhaps the most far-reaching implication of Carlyle's broadened conception of heroism is its decoupling of heroic achievement from the willingness to risk one's life. Some of Carlyle's "Great Men" have indeed done so, but certainly not all. Whatever the achievement of a Shakespeare or a Samuel Johnson, grave danger to the person of each was not part of the pursuit of it.

Carlyle says "the Thoughts" of "Great Men" underlie all human accomplishment. Here, the deeds of the classical hero are subordinate to the conception that precedes them in the hero's mind. It is indeed somewhat easier to connect the respective achievement of an Aristotle and a Caesar by conceptualizing both as beginning in the mind, whether as a vision of where to go or the determination to begin going there (which Nietzsche would soon characterize as the "will to power"). But there is a difference between writing a book and conquering the world. There are indeed circumstances in which writing a book is dangerous. Aleksandr Solzhenitsyn knew the risk he was running in secretly writing his chronicle of the Soviet prison system, *The Gulag Archipelago*. Though Solzhenitsyn's is an extreme case, many other writers have had occasion to be careful lest they run afoul of political authority. Nevertheless, attempting to conquer the world is intrinsically life-threatening in a way that writing is not.

Yet once we open the door to a type of heroism that does not entail risk to life and limb, or at least a risk of persecution and imprisonment à la Solzhenitsyn, there will be no shortage of volunteers seeking to pass through it, very few of them Solzhenitsyns. In this sense, far from suffering from a dearth of heroes and of the willingness to pay appropriate respect to them, in fact, the modern world is awash in heroes, many if not most of them celebrated beyond all reason. Movie stars, athletes, and pop singers command attention and affection as never before. In the age of mass culture, Frank Sinatra, Joe DiMaggio, Elvis, the Beatles—they were like unto gods in terms of capturing the fancy of an adoring public. Of course humans being prone to disagreement, many people hated one or all of them. But even the hatred was an artifact of their ability to compel attention. Mass-scale phenomena they remained. Did Carlyle miss a couple of categories of hero to go along with kings, poets and priests? For example, entertainers and athletes?

But to be fair, not all such risk-free heroes, if heroes they are, are merely celebrities, famous chiefly for their success at the intersection of commerce and culture. Many retain a connection to heroism of a Carlylian sort—the originators of the "things that we see standing accomplished" in the political and social world. Barack Obama was certainly a hero to millions. So was John Paul II. Teddy Kennedy. George W. Bush. Osama bin Laden (though that's a more complicated story).

Yet there is also something distinctly unheroic about most modern-world heroes. The desire people feel to lift them up seems often to be accompanied by an equal and opposite desire to bring them down. Sinatra had quite a set of pipes, but his appetite for an expensive sort of low-life behavior—eating ham and eggs off the chest of a Las Vegas prostitute, for example—although distinctive, was not admirable. Tiger Woods had an equivalent talent and, it turned out, a similar propensity.

Many are the venues today where people gush over the famous. Equally important, however, are the venues devoted to proving that idols have feet of clay. Often, they are the same venues, though some seem to specialize in one side or the other of the process, either the building up or tearing down. The weekly celebrity glossies such as *People* and *Us* celebrate you, and the weekly supermarket tabloids such as the *National Enquirer* pick you apart. Don't worry, though: The weekly glossies will be there for you to herald your comeback. You can pose tastefully nude for the cover of *Vanity Fair* today, then get captured in a bikini by telephoto lens with your cellulite rippling tomorrow.

"You're ridin' high in April / shot down in May," as Ol' Blue Eyes sang. That's life. No heroic *status* attaches itself to the celebrity-heroes of modern culture, no iconography in which all of a person's actions, great and terrible alike, come across as fundamentally superior to those of lesser mortals. Heroes are a mixture of some form of greatness and an all-too-human baseness, about which people are equally if not more curious.

In the case of political figures, the partisan character of politics ensures that at least 25 percent of the population will be willing to believe and repeat the worst about a politician from the opposing camp: George W. Bush knew about the 9/11 attacks in advance; Barack Obama covered up his foreign birth. After the party nominating conventions in 2008, one could plausibly see both Barack Obama and John McCain as heroic figures: Obama as the first black man to be nominated for president, McCain for his years enduring torture in a North Vietnamese POW camp. Yet a Venn diagram of the population mapping those who regarded Obama as a hero and those regarding McCain as a hero would surely have shown very little overlap. Partisan sentiment more often than not dictates or at least temporarily overrides judgments of character.

Largely via the world of politics, we come upon another distinctly modern type of pseudohero: the *hero-victim*. Sarah Palin lost her 2008 bid to become vice president of the United States. Nevertheless, the ridicule and derision her political opponents heaped on her served also to elevate her in the eyes of her admirers. She became, for a while in the aftermath, a politico-media superstar, a best-selling author and much-sought speaker, commentator, and rabble-rouser. The allure and rewards of the stance of hero-victim were so great that Palin chose to cut short any realistic possibility of further pursuing public office by resigning the governorship of Alaska in the middle of her term. The short-term celebrity beckoning her overrode any internal inclination she might have had to strive for greater political achievement. She quit politics for Fox News.

Former Vice President Dan Quayle, who was similarly belittled while in office, once said of his critics, to the delight of his supporters, "I wear their scorn as a badge of honor." Although as I recall the occasion, Quayle sounded more than a little sententious, and thus phony, in claiming for himself this particular honor, his speechwriter's turn of phrase captured the phenomenon perfectly: The scorn of one's enemies becomes, in its own right, a symbol of a certain kind of achievement. More concisely—albeit in an Orwellian vein, if not indeed in a full-scale Nietzschean transvaluation—scorn *is* honor.

When Al Gore entitled his doomsday-flecked environmentalist documentary film *An Inconvenient Truth*, he was plucking the same hero-victim strings. He presented himself as a man who dares speak truth to power. Power, in his model, clearly doesn't want to hear the truth. Or does it? The film ranks 10th on the list of top-grossing documentaries of all time. Gore has become a very wealthy man since leaving the vice presidency, and he shared the Nobel Peace Prize in 2007. Such riches and accolades are indicia *of* power, not of someone who was ever at risk of persecution on account of being on the outs with the powerful.

Indeed, it's hard to keep track of the staggering number of people who have taken to the airwaves, the worldwide web, and the public prints in recent decades to proclaim that their enemies are trying to silence them. They present themselves as speaking out at great personal risk: perhaps to their very lives, and certainly to their livelihood and reputation. But really? In 1776, when the signers of the Declaration of Independence pledged to one another "our Lives, our Fortunes, and our sacred Honor," they really were risking everything; if George III had managed to hold on to his American colonies, they would all surely have been hanged. Neither Gore nor Palin was at risk of any such fate. On the contrary, they made millions.

In their selection and depiction of heroes, those engaged in the creation and dissemination of the cultural products of the modern world, high and low—books, movies, television programs, plays— have often conferred upon certain professions a privileged status in relation to truth-telling. Thus we have had portraits of heroic doctors who speak up about the risk of deadly plague. We have had portraits of professors who are uniquely wise in guiding us through encounters with the unknown and terrifying. (Bram Stoker's Abraham van Helsing, vampire hunter, was a doctor *and* a professor.) We have had portraits (including self-portraits!) of heroic scientists who know enough about the secrets of the universe to instruct us on all aspects of daily life, or at least that there is/are no God/gods. We have had portraits of heroic journalists unwilling to settle for less than the truth, and of heroic lawyers determined to call out in court those who are lying, and of heroic policemen and private investigators unwilling to rest until they identify the perpetrators and bring them to justice. Portraits of heroic whistleblowers describe the personal sacrifice sometimes entailed in making public what powerful interests want to keep quiet. Sometimes heroism resides not in the knowing and telling but in the seeking, as for example the conviction of heroic investigators of the paranormal and extraterrestrial that "the truth is out there."

These heroic figures appear in juxtaposition with official or powerful or popular opinion that affords them little or no respect, usually for self-interested reasons—until (perhaps) all becomes clear in the end. We the consumers of these cultural products come to appreciate the truth and the heroism of its bearers earlier than the powers-that-be, thanks to our access via dramatic narrative to the inside story of the truth-tellers as it unfolds. The success of these projects depends entirely on our identification with the motives and virtue of the truth-tellers, which is, of course, where the sympathies of the creators of these works lie.

In Henrik Ibsen's 1882 play, *An Enemy of the People*, Dr. Thomas Stockmann stumbles upon the horrible truth about the bath waters of his resort town in Norway on the eve of the tourist season: wastewater from the local tannery has contaminated the baths and will make people gravely sick. Dr. Stockmann approaches his brother, the mayor, about the problem, but the mayor rebuffs him so as not to disrupt the tourist trade. The doctor then takes his case public, to the residents of the town, who likewise fear for their livelihood. Collectively, they brand the doctor "an enemy of the people." He remains defiant in his defense of the truth to the end.

Ibsen's play seems today antidemocratic and therefore dated. Surely the reason for this, which Ibsen did not anticipate, is that modern democracies have in fact welcomed a strong dose of the administrative and regulatory state, where technocratic expertise largely prevents failures of the kind the play depicts. But meanwhile, the truth-telling likes of Dr. Stockmann have become stock figures of middlebrow morality tales.

One of the most successful television dramas of the age of mass culture was *M*A*S*H*, set in an American field hospital during the Korean War. The hero is a surgeon called Hawkeye Pierce, whom the show represents as having unique insight into humanity as a result of his daily bloody encounter with the carnage of war. We have assessed the emergence of this up-close-and-personal view of war as an element of a broader effort to discredit the pursuit of glory through slaying on the battlefield. *M*A*S*H* was certainly in that mold. Hawkeye's medical expertise transmogrifies into expertise about the human condition as such. It need hardly be said that the doctor harbors no illusions about the glory of war; war is simply a waste. Senior military commanders are mostly buffoons, if not maniacal and worse.

And it is perhaps worth noting that Alan Alda, the actor who played Hawkeye to mass acclaim, took on additional artistic responsibilities for the program as time went on. He wrote or cowrote 19 episodes in the show's 11-season run and directed 32, including the finale, the single most-watched television program in history, with 105.9 million viewers. Alda also became well-known as an activist on progressive political issues, especially women's rights. And why wouldn't people listen to him? He played a doctor of unique sensitivity, compassion, and insight. What more could one want as authority to speak out?

Come to think of it, in depicting for us the truth-teller in all his or her righteousness—in telling the truth, that is, about telling the truth—the creators of these works would seem to be presenting themselves as the greatest truth-tellers of all, and therefore the most heroic. It strikes me that many in Hollywood harbor such a vision of themselves. Certainly this is nothing new. In Plato's dialogue, *Ion*, Socrates engages in conversation with a very popular but rather stupid actor. In typically Socratic fashion, Socrates leads his confused interlocutor into the position of claiming that he, Ion, has all the skill of a great military general because he, Ion, plays generals so well on stage.

Ibsen the playwright's identification with his hero Dr. Stockmann stands at close to 100 percent—again, making Ibsen perhaps an even greater truth-teller, at least in the estimation of Ibsen. But not just Ibsen: George Bernard Shaw, a slightly younger contemporary, was another playwright brimming with the spirit of truth-telling, as well as the socialist reform agenda of the Fabian Society. Shaw regarded the three greatest playwrights ever as Shakespeare, Ibsen, and Shaw. But whatever else one may say about Shakespeare, he never created a character as didactic as Thomas Stockmann or the folks who take center stage to speak the truth in Shaw's plays—or rather, when Shakespeare created such a didact, Polonius in *Hamlet* being the prime example, the character was never Shakespeare's literary spokesman; the intention was comic.

It is interesting that we have so many more fictional examples of truth-telling heroism than we have widely recognized actual truth-telling heroes. These missing real-world examples point to the deformation to which this type of heroism is subject. In some instances, one must ask: How great, really, was the risk in speaking up? Suffice it to say that as a matter of anecdotal impression, the number of those who portray themselves or would like to be portrayed as heroic or courageous in speaking up seems far to exceed the number of cases in which the risk was genuinely high—say, imprisonment, exile, or social ostracism. In such cases, heroism loses all connection in actuality to its classical origins in risk-taking of a high order.

Now we have entered the age of wikiculture, where the requirements of notoriety and celebrity have been reduced still further thanks to differentiation and specialization: One need not be a hero to all to be a hero to some. The Internet allows fanciers of almost any specialty to aggregate and to sort themselves, and by a voluntary process to crown champions. On Twitter, @MileyCyrus has 16 million-plus followers at this writing; @JustinBieber, nearly 50 million. Now, those are mass followings by the reckoning of any times. Yet among certain members of the pundit class, 30,000 followers is quite a respectable haul, and the journalist @ezraklein, at 400,000 plus, is a bankable media commodity.

What's more, the openness of wikiculture means that dissenters are no longer out of luck: They have ample opportunity to band together to elevate a rival—as well as to denigrate the currently famous. One can accordingly speak of the "democratization" of the heroic figure: people have the right and the capability to determine who their heroes are as never before.

It is noteworthy that for most of the thousands of years of "hero worship" leading up to Carlyle's coining the term, and in many places thereafter down to the present, the "veneration" he cites as the legitimate due of heroes was not voluntary but mandatory, and there could be grave repercussions for a failure to fulfill one's duties. An "official" opinion on the subject of who counted as great or heroic prevailed, often under penalty of death or exile. This was especially true when heroic gods were involved—beings believed to have the capacity to intervene and harm mere mortal humans in the event of impiety. Socrates had to drink the hemlock after being convicted on a two-count indictment: corrupting Athenian youth and refusing to believe in the gods of the city. Alcibiades was convicted in absentia and sentenced to death for mutilating statues of Hermes. And this was all in freewheeling, democratic Athens. Imagine Sparta. What is the fate of Sodom but a warning about the danger of misbehavior in the eyes of an all-powerful and angry god?

And if the king ruled by divine right, then his person was due something akin to worship or veneration. Woe betide the commoner arrogating to himself the right of dissent. Carlyle seems to see historically—and seek contemporaneously—a consensus judgment within a people about who their heroes are. If there have been such collective judgments (which does not go without saying), the consensus was not entirely voluntary but enforced. In unfree conditions, the heroes are exactly those whom the authorities decree them to be.

In conditions of freedom, the human tendency to disagree quickly breaks up such artificial uniformity. If there is an established church, no one may go elsewhere, and God is Who the ecclesiastical authorities say He is, with the properties they deem Him to have. If the church is disestablished or the custodians of its doctrine become irresolute, all of a sudden there is a competing religion or two.

Freedom dethrones claims of superiority that hold sway by force. A doctrine of equality rebels against claims of a permanent *status* of superiority. Both to the good. The people will decide who their heroes are, if any. But contra Carlyle, they do not need to agree and in fact in most cases will not agree on who counts as heroic or as possessing a legitimate claim to some kind of superiority. The people decide, but there never comes a moment at which one can say *the people have decided*.

There are two reasons for this, one old, one new. The first and older is the fact that the judgment of the people is subject to continuous revision, and they are accountable to no one but themselves. This ability to revise one's views has its ups and downs. On one hand, it allows for adaptation to changing circumstances, which is good. On the other, the whims of the *demos* can create considerable confusion and political complexity. Shakespeare, drawing on Plutarch, depicts exactly this problem in the opening scene of *Julius Caesar*. Two tribunes, who in the Roman system are the representatives of the common people, hate Caesar and his arrogation to himself of supreme power in Rome. When they observe the people in a frenzy of adoration for Caesar, the tribunes rebuke them for hypocrisy, noting that the very same plebeians once cheered for Pompey the Great, the hero Caesar defeated in attaining supreme power: "And do you now strew flowers in his way / That comes in triumph over Pompey's blood? / Be gone!" (Act 1, scene 1, 55–57). Thus spits Marullus.

Shakespeare's view of the judgment of the common man is itself a matter of complexity; although it does not end with skepticism and contempt, it begins there. The distance between Shakespeare and Tocqueville on the subject is an indication not only of the march of the spirit of equality, but also a reminder that governance in the modern world, though indisputably democratic, has constitutional or constitutive qualities that allow it to operate at some remove from the mere vagaries of public opinion in the *demos*. We can all be thankful for that.

The modern reason we can't say *the people have decided* has to do with the richness of wikiculture. In democracy, the majority rules. In wikiculture, no group rules over another. Individuals affiliate themselves voluntarily into collectivities based on shared judgments. Wikiculture is all about clicking "like," deciding to "friend" or "follow," and registering to post on a comment board or blog. In doing so, one declares one's membership in a virtual community and agrees to abide by its rules. Now, Facebook has a page called "We Love Miley Cyrus" as well as a page called "I Hate Miley Cyrus." It so happens that the "Hate" page had 16,400 "likes" at this writing and the "Love" page a mere 4,264. But this in no way means that the Miley-haters are winning. The precise relationship between the two pages is: none whatsoever. They tell us nothing about Miley Cyrus or her status. They adjudicate or decide nothing except who "likes" them by clicking "like." They are, in their way, entirely separate worlds.

Community by affiliation certainly has its darker side. To pick an extreme example, terrorist organizations take advantage of wikiculture to find like-minded individuals and recruit them to the cause. At a less malevolent but still troubling level, if people get used to affiliating with one another solely on the basis of shared judgment and find this level of social interaction satisfying, they may become increasingly intolerant of those whose views differ from their own. In the old days, if you joined Ralph Kramden and Ed Norton at the Raccoon Lodge, chances are the ranks of your brother Raccoons would include a number of people whose views on various subjects differed markedly from yours. Now, however, you can tailor your virtual life into a series of encounters marked by agreement. One cause of modern-day political polarization in the United States is surely the enhanced ability of people to sort themselves by political opinion and pay attention only to those who share their views.

There would appear to be no going back, however. Robert Putnam, writing just before the dawn of wikiculture in *Bowling Alone*, noted the decline in voluntary association in modern American life. Tocqueville had made a great deal of the propensity of Americans to band together to do this and that and the other. He found it a source of great strength. The classically liberal spirit in America, in the 1840s, was as much about the ties that bind people to those "like themselves" as it was individualistic in orientation. A hundred and fifty years later, Putnam had cause to worry that the atomization of America was threatening both social cohesion and the mental health of individuals left largely on their own.

Wikiculture has brought association back with a vengeance. Wikiculture is open and free-wheeling in terms of the ability of people to affiliate, but often explicitly close-minded in setting the affinity group so formed off against the Other, whoever that might be. The fact that nothing is *ever* decided, in the view of adherents, between contesting claims or points of view discourages interchange between them and compromise among the contenders. If you don't like my hero, you don't have to tell me why; you can just join others rallying around *your* hero.

Although it seems impossible to deny that Carlyle lost the fight he picked—to persuade people to bow down before "Great Men"—it is nevertheless possible to find some vindication for him in contemporary social practice and cultural norms. Notwithstanding the leveling tendency of modern, egalitarian societies, we have not lost our regard for achievement, even if we occasionally disguise it.

The fact that the modern world has concluded that officially enforced claims of superiority must not stand, and that wherever a claim of "superiority" of one kind or another erupts, it must be interrogated for the human foibles that go along with it, does not mean that a voluntarily accepted claim to greatness or superiority or heroism is impossible. Tiger Woods is a great golfer. Sinatra could really sing. Elvis does nothing for me, but, hey—it's a free country. Professional baseball players are better at the game than anybody else. George W. Bush and Barack Obama are two of only 43 people to have become president of the United States, and though it is not quite right to say that they have risked their lives for the office, it is nevertheless true that presidents receive and seem to require a great deal of protection. No American, nor for that matter any member in good standing of the egalitarian modern world, would rightly call a would-be presidential assassin a hero. As we have discussed, the term is "villain."

As we were discussing our kids' respective high school graduations one day, a friend and colleague of mine noted that his daughter's school conferred its diplomas with no awards of honors or special prizes for achievement. It's perhaps a somewhat extreme egalitarianism by the standards of most high schools, but it reflects the school's commitment to a cherished principle. It also in no way suggests that the achievements of all of the students are equal. They were not all admitted to Harvard. Nor were the Ivy League–bound among them chosen from the ranks of the graduating class by lot. Our egalitarianism is not incompatible with sorting on the basis of various kinds of achievement, even if we remain zealous about the promotion of equality.

Nor, finally, is it the case that the redefinition, democratization and wikification of heroism has so attenuated the concept that we have no more heroes. We do—and not just heroes of the redefined, democratized, and wikified sort, but the genuine life-risking article. And not just the genuine article, but the kind who command unanimous acclaim of the sort Carlyle thought the "Great Men" deserved. In the next chapter, it will be time at last to meet the standard bearer of modern heroism, a figure in possession of a claim of superiority universally recognized in the modern world and wholly consistent with its egalitarianism.

## CHAPTER 8

# THE SAVING HERO

*Slaying vs. saving.*
*Heroism's modern iteration.*
*Origins in antiquity.*

We have observed that Achilles and Joan of Arc have no real place in the modern world, nor does the classical heroic type really turn up to claim a place. It would nevertheless be a highly incomplete picture of both heroism and the modern world to stop with that observation of incompatibility. The birth and decline of classical heroism are only the first part of the story of heroism. Although it is undeniable that the classical form of heroism is incompatible with the modern world, leaving aside history books and comic books, we should not fail to notice that heroism in another form is alive and well among us. Indeed, the more fully realized the modern world, the more sharply this other form of heroism comes into relief.

Entailing no less risk to life than its classical predecessor, this heroism differs from the classical in the character of the great deed done and the nature of the recognition earned from performing it. It is a heroism that not only manages to be compatible with the modern world of democratic and law-abiding producers and consumers peaceably inclined toward one another, but by its very action affirms and reinforces the legitimacy of that world—and in so doing provides a rebuttal of some consequence to the chief critique of the modern world, namely, that it will be home to Nietzsche's "the mediocre alone." Some people remain willing to put their lives on the line in service to a higher purpose. Their purpose has not been the classical hero's purpose, namely, the actualization of their sense of inner greatness, but—to serve others.

A short story with a personal connection:

Late one September night in 1994, a fire broke out in a house in suburban New Jersey. A family of 11 lived there. My wife's uncle, Patrolman David Robins of the Township of Ocean Police Department, was among the first on the scene. Members of the family gathered outside in a state of shock and hysteria as flames consumed the living room and started spreading throughout the house. The family assured Ptl. Robins that all members were accounted for.

Over the general din, however, he thought he heard a child screaming from inside. The parents had said everyone was out and safe. But he heard what he heard.

Time was critical. He couldn't enter the house through the front door. The flames and smoke were too thick. So he rushed to the back of the house and found a sliding glass door that was unlocked. He opened it and went in. He made his way forward, crawling for 25 feet beneath the thick layer of billowing smoke just above him. In the kitchen, he found one of the children, a six-year-old boy who had apparently wandered back into the house in confusion. The boy was unconscious. He grabbed the boy and made his way back through the smoke and flame, handing the child off to another officer and a firefighter near the back door. An ambulance took the rescued boy off to a hospital for treatment for smoke inhalation. He made a full recovery. Ptl. Robins had saved his life.

This is the modern face of heroism—someone willing to take a tremendous risk or make a personal sacrifice for the sake of others.

The firefighters who rushed into the World Trade Center towers the morning of 9/11 must have known they were going to have a hard day, maybe their worst ever. They were not deluded. No doubt each one hoped to live to see the next day, as did my wife's uncle, a man of great personal charm and bonhomie and no death wish whatsoever. But entering a burning building is no way to improve your chances, something he and the 9/11 firefighters understood on their hardest day and on previous days of danger, when things turned out all right. Their ability and willingness to undertake such a feat entailed physical and moral courage, the discipline and the training that underlie it, a willingness to act selflessly, and an instant determination that overcame hesitation and the impulse to do what most people in such circumstances would do, namely, run the other way.

Meanwhile, heroic doctors and other volunteers from *Medecins san Frontieres* have risked their own lives in or near zones of civil war, conflict, and epidemic to treat the wounded, injured, and sick on an impartial basis. Some volunteers have been killed, others kidnapped and taken hostage. Aid workers from numerous other humanitarian organizations have stepped into hotspots worldwide in service to those most desperately in need.

Sèrgio Viera de Mello had a brilliant career as an international civil servant at the United Nations cut tragically short by a bomb blast in Iraq. Viera de Mello represented the office of the United Nations High Commissioner for Refugees in Mozambique during the civil war following independence in 1975, in Lebanon during the conflict in the early 1980s, in central Africa dealing with refugee crises, in Cambodia and extensively in Yugoslavia during the years it was breaking apart. He oversaw the reconstruction effort in East Timor following its war of independence from Sri Lanka. Samantha Power's 2008 biography of Viera de Mello was aptly entitled *Sergio: One Man's Fight to Save the World*. He became the UN High Commissioner for Human Rights and was widely mentioned as a potential future secretary-general when he accepted the assignment as the UN's top official in Iraq following the fall of the Saddam Hussein regime. The danger posed by the mounting Iraqi insurgency eluded UN planners on the scene, and their headquarters in the Canal Hotel was destroyed by a suicide truck bomb, killing Viera de Mello and 21 others and wounding more than 100.

The deeds of many lifesaving heroes have gone unsung, but sometimes their achievements are so extraordinary they have won worldwide acclaim. Chesley "Sully" Sullenberger was the U.S. Airways pilot who performed the first perfect "water landing" in the history of commercial aviation by setting his plane down safely on the Hudson River in January 2009. Sully had a powerful personal interest in the success of his efforts: He had his own life to save as well as those of all his passengers and crew. Yet the sheer technical virtuosity of the achievement, the evident grace under extreme pressure, the perfection of the result, and the number of people who might well have died in that plane that day together made out a special case of the life-saving hero: supreme competence in near-impossible conditions.

Battlefields continue to be places of heroism, but not only for vanquishing the enemy in the style of Julius Caesar and Timur the Great. The history of the Congressional Medal of Honor charts an evolution in the kind of action deemed worthy of the U.S. military's highest decoration. The fact that the number of citations awarded posthumously has increased over time is somewhat well-known. The highest decoration doesn't *require* what Abraham Lincoln called "the last full measure of devotion," but exceptionally meritorious action in the course of which one loses one's life is the norm. The Congressional Medal of Honor is not something one plausibly sets out to win. Also, the number of citations in relation to the number of Americans serving in wartime has declined over time, making the award all the more rare.

In general, all the awards (as one would expect) entail voluntary action that increases the risk to one's life. Beyond that, there are two broad narratives that appear in the citations. In one, the honoree takes heroic action that results in the death or capture of the enemy (single-handedly charging the enemy pillboxes and engaging in hand-grenade duels to silence the gunfire from them, for example). In the other, the honoree takes heroic action that saves the life or lives of a fellow service member (exposing oneself to fire to retrieve a wounded comrade, for example; the limit case is surely diving on a grenade in order to absorb the explosion, saving those nearby). Of course, in some citations, both narratives are present.

Over time, the percentage of citations that include a saving narrative has increased markedly. My researcher, Ben Atlas, reviewed Medal of Honor citations from the creation of the award during the Civil War to the present, classifying each of them on a 1–5 scale based on the extent to which the saving of lives figures into the citation. Here is the scale:

1—Citations with no reference at all to rescuing or otherwise assisting a comrade. This rating includes actions such as capturing a flag (frequently found in the Civil War citations), simply killing enemy combatants or otherwise disrupting the enemy, and allowing U.S. arms to advance successfully.

2—Citations that imply actions of "saving" heroism but do not mention such action explicitly. These include citations that involve shipping rations and supplies to fellow soldiers or leading troops so a mission is achieved "with a minimum of casualties."

3—Citations that explicitly mention some form of rescuing or saving but emphasize some other aspect of the laureate's gallantry. This category would include actions such as a soldier administering first aid to a fallen comrade before proceeding to kill 25 enemy combatants.

4—The inverse of 3: citations in which the "saving" action is the focus and emphasis, but other elements are still present. For example, a citation describing a soldier who killed two enemy combatants, then went on to sacrifice his life to save the remainder of his platoon by covering a grenade with his body.

5—Citations that refer only to saving action. It should be noted that background information included in the citation was not taken into account. If the citation explains that a soldier was fighting in a certain battle against a certain enemy when he jumped on top of a grenade, that citation falls in this category.

Here is an example from World War I of a citation classified 1. It describes the extraordinary valor of Samuel Woodfill, who is generally regarded as the most decorated soldier of the war:

> While he was leading his company against the enemy, his line came under heavy machinegun fire, which threatened to hold up the advance. Followed by 2 soldiers at 25 yards, this officer went out ahead of his first line toward a machinegun nest and worked his way around its flank, leaving the 2 soldiers in front. When he got within 10 yards of the gun it ceased firing, and 4 of the enemy appeared, 3 of whom were shot by 1st Lt. Woodfill. The fourth, an officer, rushed at 1st Lt. Woodfill, who attempted to club the officer with his rifle. After a hand-to-hand struggle, 1st Lt. Woodfill killed the officer with his pistol. His company thereupon continued to advance, until shortly afterwards another machinegun nest was encountered. Calling on his men to follow, 1st Lt. Woodfill rushed ahead of his line in the face of heavy fire from the nest, and when several of the enemy appeared above the nest he shot them, capturing 3 other members of the crew and silencing the gun. A few minutes later this officer for the third time demonstrated conspicuous daring by charging another machinegun position, killing 5 men in one machinegun pit with his rifle. He then drew his revolver and started to jump into the pit, when 2 other gunners only a few yards away turned their gun on him. Failing to kill them with his revolver, he grabbed a pick lying nearby and killed both of them. Inspired by the exceptional courage displayed by this officer, his men pressed on to their objective under severe shell and machinegun fire.

And here is an example from the Afghanistan war, a posthumous citation honoring Jared C. Monti, classified 4 on our rating scale:

Staff Sergeant Jared C. Monti distinguished himself by acts of gallantry and intrepidity above and beyond the call of duty while serving as a team leader with Headquarters and Headquarters Troop, 3d Squadron, 71st Cavalry Regiment, 3d Brigade Combat Team, 10th Mountain Division, in connection with combat operations against an armed enemy in Nuristan Province, Afghanistan, on June 21, 2006. While Staff Sergeant Monti was leading a mission aimed at gathering intelligence and directing fire against the enemy, his 16-man patrol was attacked by as many as 50 enemy fighters. On the verge of being overrun, Staff Sergeant Monti quickly directed his men to set up a defensive position behind a rock formation. He then called for indirect fire support, accurately targeting the rounds upon the enemy who had closed to within 50 meters of his position. While still directing fire, Staff Sergeant Monti personally engaged the enemy with his rifle and a grenade, successfully disrupting an attempt to flank his patrol. Staff Sergeant Monti then realized that one of his Soldiers was lying wounded in the open ground between the advancing enemy and the patrol's position. With complete disregard for his own safety, Staff Sergeant Monti twice attempted to move from behind the cover of the rocks into the face of relentless enemy fire to rescue his fallen comrade. Determined not to leave his Soldier, Staff Sergeant Monti made a third attempt to cross open terrain through intense enemy fire. On this final attempt, he was mortally wounded, sacrificing his own life in an effort to save his fellow Soldier. Staff Sergeant Monti's selfless acts of heroism inspired his patrol to fight off the larger enemy force. Staff Sergeant Monti's immeasurable courage and uncommon valor are in keeping with the highest traditions of military service and reflect great credit upon himself, Headquarters and Headquarters Troop, 3rd Squadron, 71st Cavalry Regiment, 3rd Brigade Combat Team, 10th Mountain Division, and the United States Army.

The trend line is unmistakable. Average ratings of classifications for citations awarded in wars and major conflicts have increased dramatically over time. From the Civil War to World War I, the average rating of citations rose from 1.4 to 2.3. The World War II average was very close to that of World War I. Citations during the Korean War, however, averaged just over 2.8. The average for Vietnam-era citations increased still further, to nearly 3.6, and citations for Iraq averaged 4.5.

It is by no means certain that more life-saving goes on on the battlefield today than took place in previous times. Nor is it clear that the actual conduct on the battlefield meriting the nation's highest honor has actually changed. It would likely be possible, for example, to rewrite Lt. Woodfill's citation to incorporate reference to how his actions saved the lives of his comrades. It is also certainly possible that some of the apparent increase in the premium attached to the saving of lives in the awarding of Congressional Medals of Honor is a product of the changing character of the battlefield or other external influences. Nevertheless, the increasing emphasis on life-saving activity over time is so starkly apparent that it is tempting to conclude that no one will get the Congressional Medal of Honor any more simply for exacting a price on the enemy. Absent the saving function, the chance of a medal being awarded now seems vanishingly low.

If the military itself—indeed, the most powerful military in the world, but notably the military of a power long steeped in the egalitarianism of modernity—now designates its highest heroes not on the basis of their infliction of violent death on an enemy but on the saving of lives, then we have perhaps reached the point in the development of the modern world at which the modern, saving form of heroism has eclipsed the vestigial forms of classical heroism and their slaying ways for good. This is not to say that slaying is no longer necessary or, in the proper context, appropriate and even worthy of praise. But the *necessity* of slaying is regrettable; the military itself seems to have incorporated at least that much of the twentieth-century critique of the pursuit of glory on the battlefield.

Life-saving is at the heart of the vignettes *Newsweek* included in its edition of November 12, 2012, dubbed "The Heroes Issue." It was published shortly after Hurricane Sandy devastated the New Jersey coast and as the tempo of U.S. operations in Afghanistan was near its peak. The magazine offers many inspiring stories, some of them harrowing. One tells of a Coast Guard rescue swimmer making his way through 30-foot seas to save a man who had fallen off a life boat after abandoning ship in the storm. Another recreates the amazing feats of DUSTOFF 73, an Army ambulance corps helicopter and its crew, who over 48 hours in Afghanistan's "Valley of Death" in Kunar province, amid heavy fighting on the ground in June 2011 and difficult weather in the sky, rescued 14 wounded Americans, recovered two bodies, and ran three resupply runs, nearly getting killed themselves in the process.

Not all the stories in *Newsweek*'s "Heroes Issue" involve risk to one's own life: some are about people called on in difficult circumstances to work tirelessly around the clock to ensure that others get to safety. But many certainly do entail that risk, as in the case of members of Team Rubicon, a nonprofit established and staffed by veterans of Iraq and Afghanistan, who mobilize to provide relief in disaster situations. Two such members, former active duty Marines, took it upon themselves to round up a boat and guide it through chest-deep flood waters to rescue a man trapped in his attic in Gerritsen Beach, Brooklyn, after Sandy made landfall.

To risk one's life to save a stranger is to place a very high value indeed on the life of the stranger: a value equal to if not greater than the value one place's on one's own life. You have voluntarily embraced a situation in which the outcome may be the stranger's survival and your demise, when by doing nothing, the outcome—as certain as one can ever be about such things—is your survival. *You are unwilling to privilege your very life over a stranger's life*: I submit that this is the ultimate expression of the spirit of equality.

The hero as slayer versus the hero as lifesaver: That is the crux of the difference between the classical and the modern form of heroism. Greatness versus equality. Ego versus generosity. "I am someone" versus "I can do something for someone."

No differently from their classical counterparts, life-saving heroes are willing to risk death. The significance of this fact cannot be overstated, especially in the parts of the world where the *routine* exposure of human beings to the danger of violent death has gone away. The modern world is, generally speaking, peaceable and devoted to thoroughly bourgeois pursuits. Safety, comfort, and pleasure are for most people today as much as they want. Yet safety, comfort, and pleasure have *always* been, for most people, as much as they want. The modern world differs from the classical world chiefly in delivering those goods more broadly—indeed, on a mass scale.

The critics of bourgeois modernity have held, contemptuously, that safety and comfort are all there is to the modern world. The intention of the critique that Nietzsche, Jünger, the twentieth-century philosopher Martin Heidegger, and others propagated was to preserve a vision of a higher type of human life than one organized around pleasure and gain. Nietzsche had his imaginary Superman. Jünger foresaw and ever-so-cautiously applauded a fascist social order in which individuals would understand and embrace their duty to sacrifice themselves for the state or *Das Volk*. Heidegger sought philosophical refuge in a rejection of the Cartesian individualism of Western metaphysics and a radical confrontation with Being.

At the core of these critiques are two factual claims, one of which turns out to be misleading in context, and the other of which is simply false. The first is that, as Tocqueville noted, the spirit of egalitarianism had become pervasive, and it was producing a type of society in which people thought of others as "like themselves." This claim is true. Hence the birth of the Hobbesian idea that government has its origins in the voluntary association of individuals seeking protection for themselves. Hence the powerful attraction of the idea of a contract, a transaction between two parties in which both potentially benefit. Hence the exciting ideas bubbling forth in the eighteenth century about individual "rights" stemming from a common humanity, not as a grant from political powers. Hence democratic government (perhaps more properly, small-R republican government). Hence, finally, the emergence in stable, capitalist, democratic polities of the safety-, pleasure-, and comfort-seeking bourgeoisie as the universal class.

But although the claim about the pervasiveness of individualistic egalitarianism is true, those complaining about it are generally insufficiently appreciative of the readily discernible desire of most people, most of the time, and for most all of time, for exactly this kind of life. Thomas Hobbes did not invent the bourgeois spirit; he described something he took to be a general and perhaps permanent characteristic of most people, and therefore one whose origin lay not in modern times but in the farthest reach of antiquity, the "state of nature." Machiavelli had a characteristically economical and witty way of saying the same thing: that a prince can avoid the considerable danger of being hated by the people if "he abstains from the property of his citizens and his subjects, and from their women" (XVII). Machiavelli here reduces the majority of human aspiration to the wish to be left alone: first, implicitly, from all other would-be predators and marauders of the state of nature à la Hobbes, protection from which is the job of the prince; second, once he has established conditions of public order, from the prince himself.

So we have a *general* desire on the part of most human beings for a quiet life, not a uniquely modern desire. True, politics has often, if not mostly, thwarted this desire, but in the modern world mostly does not. The successful fulfillment of this desire tells us something important about the character of the modern world, namely, that *the desire for a quiet life is not an irrational or impossible desire in all cases*. In fact, the fulfillment of this desire on a broad scale is a kind of culminating position of political order. But this fulfillment tells us nothing about the relative prevalence of the desire for a quiet life in modern times compared to past times.

I am in fact prepared to stipulate that such desire is indeed more prevalent now. But that's because so many people used to suppress it—or never used to entertain it in the first place—on the grounds that a quiet life was completely unrealistic. A young man born in early fourteenth-century Central Asia might well decide to go all-in and enjoy the marauding ways of the Golden Horde to the hilt of both his sword and his cock. In terms of his life choices, however, there was no point at which the suburbs were beckoning. Yet Hobbes's view of this desire as *latently* widespread from the time of the origin of the human seems well-founded.

Was this latent desire corrosive, somehow working slowly over tens of centuries to create the modern world by eliminating the rule of the strong, the divine right of kings, and hereditary aristocratic privilege? This is the story of modernity as moderns usually tell it. Of course, most moderns tell it sympathetically, as a story of uplift.

Yet this is the same story Nietzsche tells from the opposite perspective: the loss of the higher possibilities of the human in a slough of mediocrity. As we have seen, what remains ultimately mysterious in this account is exactly *how high* these higher possibilities of the human could have been if they were so readily undermined by the presumably lower desire for a 40-hour workweek, a good cup of coffee, 400 cable television channels, and the like—the things most people choose when they have the freedom to choose.

Our project here, to better understand heroism and therefore, it turns out, the development of political order, has come to see political order and change as a series of responses on the part of its custodians to the possible emergence of challengers to it. I am in accord with the modern propensity to see this change as "evolutionary," in the sense of possessing a directionality—from rule by the strongest, to kingly rule, to feudal and aristocratic order, to politics driven by the spirit of equality. The story as we have been looking at it, however, does not require a notional corrosive agent acting as a hidden hand. All it requires, in the first instance, is a strong individual seeking to avoid dominance by another strong individual. This seems to me to be prehistoric in origin but eminently an actual element of human history, and not one humans have fully passed beyond, as some of today's struggles demonstrate. The efforts of self-preservation on the part of strong individuals have sometimes succeeded but sometimes have not, giving rise to new efforts on behalf of the maintenance of political order—and eventually entailing more elaborate efforts to the same end, and therefore more elaborate political order, but still intermittent failure. The most elaborate effort so far, and the one with the most promise for stability, is the modern, democratic, egalitarian world.

So what has happened to Nietzsche's higher human type, the heroic type? Nietzsche and many others have lamented the passing of this type from the scene, regarding our human prospects as accordingly diminished. It's this claim, I submit, that is all wrong. The heroic type we still have with us.

The type has never been common among human beings, though there was once a time when people routinely found themselves in situations where they would have to fight or die, and perhaps the challenge drew out the heroic in some, even many, who would otherwise have been content with a quiet life, were one available. In the modern world, of course, people are not routinely pressed into such circumstances. Yet some still seek them out. They become Navy SEALs and Army Rangers, maybe cops and firefighters. Or they live ordinary, quiet lives until something rare and spectacular gets set in their path, at which time they choose to do what most people, often including most or all of those in their immediate proximity, do not: jump in the river to try to pull a stranger out after a plane crash; charge the cockpit once it becomes clear the 9/11 hijackers plan to crash the plane into a building.

Unlike their classical counterparts, life-saving heroes pose no threat to modern political order. These actual individuals have achieved their greatness not for self-aggrandizement, but through helping others. Far from being subversive, their heroic deeds have actually served to reinforce the democratic political order of the modern world, where the principle of equality has pride of place. The great deeds heroes have performed and the great risks they have run in order to save the lives of strangers have contributed to the egalitarian ethos of the modern world by establishing that *the modern meaning of greatness is service to others.*

Though the act of lifesaving represents the pinnacle of heroic achievement in the modern world, the figure of the saving hero is nothing new under the sun: Like the slaying hero, the saving hero has origins in antiquity.

I have described Homer's *Iliad* as a portrait of the greatest of all classical heroes, Achilles—a hero in the slaying and conquering sense, acting as he deems he must (for all the trouble it causes his comrades and even in the knowledge that it will cost him his life). Homer also explores the complex relationship between heroism and the political order in his depiction of the conflict between the greatest hero and the greatest king, Agamemnon. But Homer did not quite end the heroic portraiture of the *Iliad* there. It's time for us to turn once again to the enigmatic character of Patroclus, Achilles's great friend.

I have observed that we do not really know *why* Patroclus is Achilles's best friend—what's in it for Achilles, or for that matter, for Patroclus?

The most we really hear about the origins of the bond comes from the reminiscences of old king Nestor, who was among those responsible for recruiting Achilles and Patroclus to Agamemnon's cause in the war. Nestor reminds Patroclus of the advice the two young men received from their respective fathers before setting out for Troy:

> "The old horseman Peleus urging his son Achilles,
> 'Now always be the best, my boy, the bravest,
> and hold your head up high above the others.'
> and . . . Menoetius urging you [Patroclus], 'My child,
> Achilles is nobler than you with his immortal blood
> but you are older. He has more power than you, by far,
> but give him sound advice, guide him, even in battle.
> Achilles will listen to you—for his own good.'" (XI 935–941)

Without contesting Achilles's pride of place—Achilles "is nobler"—Patroclus's father nevertheless insists that Patroclus has something Achilles needs: good counsel—even in the extreme circumstances of battle, when the greatest warrior is in his element. Achilles, Menoetius says, will listen to Patroclus's advice "for his own good," which is to say, not merely to indulge Patroclus, but because Patroclus can provide Achilles with something the latter is unable to find within himself. Achilles's heroism or greatness or nobility, that which makes him "the best," is not self-sufficient in terms of wisdom. He could still use some advice from time to time.

In recalling to Patroclus this episode of fatherly guidance, Nestor himself is not at all disinterested. He thinks the outcome of the war, and thus the future of Greek civilization, hangs on whether Achilles will fight. Nestor wants Patroclus to advise Achilles to rejoin the battle. And seemingly speaking on the fly, as it occurs to him, Nestor offers a second-best proposal to Patroclus:

> at least let Achilles send *Patroclus* into battle.
> Let the whole Myrmidon army follow your command—
> you might bring some light of victory to our Argives!
> And let him give you his own fine armor to wear in war
> so the Trojans might take *you* for him, Patroclus, yes,
> hold off from attack, and Achaea's fighting sons
> get second wind, exhausted as they are . . .
> [. . .] you could roll those broken Trojans back to Troy . . . (XI 951–960)

The Homeric epithet associated with Patroclus, in the mouth of the poet himself and of his characters, is "amiable" or "gentle." It is used of no other character in the *Iliad*. As a result of his consultation with Nestor, "the fighting spirit leapt inside Patroclus" and "he dashed back by the ships toward Achilles." The impression is that of a man single-mindedly on a mission. But en route, Patroclus comes upon a wounded Achaean fighter. He tarries to tend to the wounds. The benevolent generosity of Patroclus, which distinguishes him from the other Achaean warriors, trumps the surge of "fighting spirit" when confronted with a wounded warrior in need of attention.

When he finally does meet up with Achilles, Patroclus is weeping for the dire straits of the Achaeans:

> Our former champions, all laid up in the ships,
> all are hit by arrows or run through by spears. (XVI 26–27)

He exhorts Achilles to return to battle, but if not—Patroclus proposes Nestor's scheme instead.

Achilles is not unmoved, and is even self-critical about absenting himself from the battle: "How on earth," he muses, "can a man rage on forever?" (XVI 70). At this point, he wants to get back in the fight. But in the absence of rectification of Agamemnon's slight to him, Achilles can't see a way to do so—not until the Trojans directly threaten the Myrmidon ships, that is, in defense of his own people, which would be too late for the rest of the Achaeans. So Achilles works a slight transformation on the aspiration underlying Nestor's plan: Patroclus will indeed lead the Myrmidons into battle, wearing Achilles's armor. He will drive the Trojans from the ships they are threatening to overrun. Then Patroclus will turn around and return. So great will the gratitude of the Achaeans be that they will give Achilles back his concubine, Briseis, redressing Agamemnon's slight. Then he, Achilles, will return to lead the Achaeans in final victory over Troy.

We must pause here to note that Achilles's plan is, not to put too fine a point on it, cockamamie. There is sense to the proposition that Patroclus, leading the fresh Myrmidon army into battle, can turn the tide against the advancing but fatigued Trojans. And perhaps Nestor is correct that Patroclus will have an additional edge if the Trojans mistake him, because of the armor he is wearing, for the much-feared Achilles.

But then what? Patroclus is supposed to turn back. And then, as Achilles imagines it, the Achaeans in gratitude will spontaneously return Briseis to Achilles. But why? Are the Achaeans also supposed to mistake

Patroclus for Achilles? That's far-fetched. Does Achilles think he will receive Briseis as his due simply because he lent Patroclus his armor and his army? Maybe. But does that give us reason to think Agamemnon will give back Achilles's prize? At the cost of Agamemnon doing without? With the Trojans routed, why wouldn't Agamemnon be more inclined to reward *Patroclus*?

The rampaging Patroclus does indeed succeed in turning back the Trojan attack. But he does not do as Achilles told him. In accordance with Nestor's version of the plan, Patroclus continues to advance on Troy. And there he dies at the hand of Hector. His last words are of Achilles, an admonition to Hector that Achilles will cut Hector down in turn. Patroclus believes his own death will bring Achilles into the battle.

He is right about that. I think it's quite possible that old Nestor's plan for Patroclus to lead the fresh Myrmidon army into battle when dressed in Achilles's armor may well have been based on the view that the Achaeans would gain either way: Either Patroclus and the Myrmidons would be so dominant on the battlefield that the Trojans would "roll . . . broken . . . back to Troy," winning the Achaeans the day—or Patroclus might die trying, in which case the prodigious and angry Achilles would surely return to the battlefield to avenge him.

But regardless of whether Nestor had it all figured out, Patroclus has a clear view in his own mind. As he lays mortally wounded, with Hector standing over him, Patroclus says:

> One more thing—take it to heart, I urge you—
> you too, you won't live long yourself, I swear.
> Already I see them looming up beside you—death
> and the strong force of fate, to bring you down
> at the hands of Aeacus' great royal son . . .
> Achilles! (XVI 996–1000)

It seems an inescapable conclusion that Patroclus knew exactly what he was doing. His own death would draw his great friend back into the battle at last. Never mind Achilles's instructions to turn back after initially repulsing the Trojan advance, in the absurd hope that Achilles would get his prize back. The direct approach offers a certain path to success. Patroclus knows that Achilles will go to war to avenge his death regardless of the status of Achilles's row with Agamemnon. Patroclus knows that Achilles is the greatest fighter. Patroclus knows how great the peril of the Achaeans is. And Patroclus knows that by risking and then sacrificing his own life, he can avert disaster.

Achilles, back in his tent, is full of foreboding. He has seen the tide of battle turn twice: first, against the Trojans, at the eleventh hour, as they were on the verge of burning the Argive ships, thanks presumably to Patroclus; now, alarmingly, back against the Achaeans. He is worried about his friend, and suddenly recalls another prophecy:

> "Dear gods, don't bring to pass the grief that haunts my heart—
> the prophecy that mother revealed to me one time . . .
> she said the best of the Myrmidons—while I lived—
> would fall at Trojan hands and leave the light of day.
> And now he's dead. I know it." (XVIII 8–12)

Gentle Patroclus is "the best of the Myrmidons"—not nobler than Achilles, not greater, but *better than* Achilles and best of all his people. That's because he understands that the only way to save the Greeks in the hour of their greatest peril is to give up his own life in the manner of the saving hero.

Of course it is not exclusively the warrior's art that reveals the saving hero. Marcus Tullius Cicero, for example, was a first century BCE philosopher and lawyer. He came to fame not on the battlefields of the relentlessly expanding Roman Empire, as did most of those who rose to the top in the Republic, but by conducting prosecutions in the Forum, a venue in which he could exercise his vast rhetorical skills to the fullest. Cicero was born into the lowest rank of the Roman aristocracy, the

Equestrian order, or knights. He was not from one of the great families of Rome. That he managed to raise himself up to the pinnacle of Roman power is testimony to the depth of his ambition and his political skill.

The Republic of the first century BCE was decadent. The expansion of territory gained by the press of Roman arms was in no danger of being checked; apart from the occasional manageable rebellion, the external security of Rome was assured. The problem was internal. The supporters and defenders of the Republic were rarely able to clearly perceive its weaknesses and contradictions, let alone to muster the resources and will to attempt needed corrections and rebalancing. Conspiracies abounded, including the one that would eventually do in the Republic, Caesar's. But before Caesar, others tried and failed. When he became consul in 63 BCE, Cicero found himself forced to deal with a conspiracy to assassinate him and overthrow the Republic led by Lucius Sergius Catilina.

In the end, Cicero succeeded in exposing the conspiracy and rounding up the principal conspirators, excluding Catilina himself, who fled Rome in response to Cicero's withering denunciation of him in the Senate. Cicero had the other conspirators hauled before the Senate, which heard them confess to the plot. Cicero then faced the exceedingly difficult problem of what to do with them.

They were Roman citizens, after all. Though consul, Cicero had no legal authority to put such men to death without a trial. Yet they were also too dangerous to be allowed to live, and trying them would pose grave risks as well. Opinion in the Roman Senate was divided: Julius Caesar spoke in opposition to the death penalty; Cato the Younger in favor. Cicero, though aware that he might one day be called to account for his extralegal decision and exiled, ordered the conspirators killed anyway, and they were strangled in their holding cells that night.

Although his political opponents later did indeed use the death sentences against him, most of his contemporaries supported him and cheered him. As a result of foiling the conspiracy and saving the Republic, the Senate conveyed upon him the title, "Pater patriae," or father of the fatherland. There had been only two previous such honorees; the first was Romulus, the quasi-mythical founder of Rome; the second, in the fourth century BCE, was Marcus Furious Camillus, who routed a Gallic army that had successfully besieged Rome and was dubbed Rome's second founder. Neither Cicero nor any other Roman, including Pompey the Great, had an answer to the problem of Julius Caesar a few years later, but before that, Cicero certainly had good claim to the mantle of saving hero.

Abraham Lincoln, too, was a lawyer of modest origin and considerable philosophical and rhetorical gifts. He, too, harbored outsized personal ambitions. Faced with the secession of the South and civil war, he framed his political task precisely in the terms we have been discussing: his great task would be to "save the Union." As he laid out the problem in his first inaugural address:

> A disruption of the Federal Union, heretofore only menaced, is now formidably attempted.
>
> I hold that in contemplation of universal law and of the Constitution the Union of these States is perpetual. Perpetuity is implied, if not expressed, in the fundamental law of all national governments. It is safe to assert that no government proper ever had a provision in its organic law for its own termination. Continue to execute all the express provisions of our National Constitution, and the Union will endure forever. . . .
>
> In *your* hands, my dissatisfied fellow-countrymen, and not in *mine*, is the momentous issue of civil war. The Government will not assail you. You can have no conflict without being yourselves the aggressors. *You* have no oath registered in heaven to destroy the Government, while I shall have the most solemn one to "preserve, protect, and defend it."

In pursuit of the task of saving the Union, Lincoln, like Cicero, was willing to step outside the bounds of the law. He suspended the venerable writ of *habeas corpus*, the requirement that the government appear in court to justify its detention of any person, to squelch those seeking to hamper the Union cause. As justification for his Emancipation Proclamation freeing the slaves in the Confederate states, he cited military necessity and his authority as commander-in-chief, a constitutional reach even in the view of many staunch opponents of slavery.

Cicero was eventually cut down by his political enemies. He knew they were after him and was on the lam, but the assassins eventually found him. This is not an especially noteworthy element of his story as a great figure of Rome, insofar as so many of his contemporaries met a similar end. Dying quietly at home was not necessarily the expectation of those who chose to engage in politics in the last years of the Roman Republic and the early years of the Roman Empire.

Eighteen centuries later in the New World, however, a political leader's death by assassination was a shocking and momentous event even in the context of an ongoing Civil War. Lincoln was, of course, woefully inattentive to his personal security. Machiavelli would not approve. His assassination on April 15, 1865, prevented him from seeing the end of the war, but by then, the outcome was not in doubt. Nor, really, did the handiwork of his killer, John Wilkes Booth, have much effect on the war one way or another. Yet supporters immediately moved to portray Lincoln as a martyr to the cause of saving the Union, and he has been the premier saving hero of American politics ever since.

One Western figure towers above all in the category of saving hero, however. That would be Jesus of Nazareth, who is called "Savior" by 2.2 billion human beings alive today. At the center of Christianity is the belief that God sent His son to earth to redeem the human race. In the famous words attributed to Jesus in the Gospel of John, "For God so loved the world, that He gave His only begotten Son, that whoever believes in Him shall not perish, but have eternal life. For God did not send the Son into the world to judge the world, but that the world might be saved through Him" (John 3:16–17). Jesus accomplished this through his death and resurrection.

The apostle Paul, in his letter to the Romans, describes the resurrection as the ultimate victory over death and sin. It was not, of course, merely a personal triumph on the part of the raised Jesus, who had no personal sin to overcome. Rather, it was the sin of the world, and all the people in it, which Jesus took upon himself. His crucifixion was something he endured entirely for the benefit of those willing to acknowledge Jesus as the Christ and Savior, so to be delivered from their sin and the just punishment it would bring in the world to come.

Raising oneself from the dead is a feat no mere human being can perform; the body is finite, and death is permanent. Jesus overcomes death once and for all by rising from the dead, thus showing others the way to life everlasting:

> [A]s Christ was raised from the dead through the glory of the Father, so we too might walk in newness of life. For if we have become united with *Him* in the likeness of His death, certainly we shall also be *in the likeness* of His resurrection, knowing this, that our old self was crucified with *Him*, in order that our body of sin might be done away with, so that we would no longer be slaves to sin; for he who has died is freed from sin. Now if we have died with Christ, we believe that we shall also live with Him, knowing that Christ, having been raised from the dead, is never to die again; death no longer is master over Him. For the death that He died, He died to sin once for all; but the life that He lives, He lives to God. (Romans 6:4–10)

Jesus thus serves as a flawless example others can aspire to emulate: willing sacrifice on behalf of others. In the first epistle attributed to the apostle Peter, the first leader of the Roman church, the author exhorts his audience that Jesus Christ

> suffered for you, leaving you an example for you to follow in His steps, who committed no sin, nor was any deceit found in His mouth; and while being reviled, He did not revile in return; while suffering, He uttered no threats, but kept entrusting *Himself* to Him who judges righteously; and He Himself bore our sins in His body on the cross, so

that we might die to sin and live to righteousness; for by His wounds you were healed. (1 Peter 2:21–24)

I have written at some length elsewhere on the content of the message Jesus conveyed about how people should get along with each other in the world, finding in the statements attributed to him a coherent case for mutual freedom and equality—and as such, the birth of the modern world. This message is mostly secondary for our purposes here; more important than what I called the Jesusian political teaching is the Christian teaching of resurrection and redemption, which is specifically aimed at the next world, not this one: securing eternal life in the presence of God. This is the "saving" that those who believe in Jesus Christ as Savior have in mind.

One element of the political teaching of Jesus, however, is of special note for our purposes in considering the relationship of heroism and politics. "Blessed are the gentle," Jesus says in the Beatitudes, the opening section of the Sermon on the Mount, "for they shall inherit the earth" (Matthew 5:5). Jesus refers here not to an otherworldly reward for the gentle or meek, but a reward in this world—in fact, the reward *of* this world to the gentle. How is that supposed to happen, exactly? The late Christopher Hitchens, with whom I sparred well into many a California summer night over religion, once gave me a T-shirt declaring, "IF YOU BELIEVE THE MEEK WILL INHERIT THE EARTH YOU'RE JUST WHERE THEY WANT YOU"—which is to say, complacently in the clutches of the powerful in the hope of divine deliverance, and therefore perpetuating the reign of the powerful.

Jesus left the meaning of the "Blessed are . . . " statements of the Beatitudes to his auditors to figure out. But on the assumption that the words of the Sermon on the Mount were carefully chosen, have a look at the modality by which the gentle come to possess the earth. It's a bequest. From whom? Presumably, those currently running it and calling the shots, often to the detriment of the gentle or meek and their wish for a quiet life. The Jesusian suggestion is that the powerful will die out as a type, leaving the world as the property of those who wish for a quiet life. This points to the Jesusian view of the ultimate instability of politics based on the rule of the strong—which is to say, a politics in which the slaying hero looms as the ultima ratio against which political order must stand, however tenuously.

A world in which the slaying hero has no place, the modern world, still leaves room for heroism of the saving kind. Thus we have Achilles and Jesus, the antipodes of heroism in the ancient and modern worlds.

In Chapter 7, we looked at the democratization and wikification of the adjudication of heroism. No coercive power enforces an official judgment of who does and who doesn't constitute a hero. The people decide for themselves. And naturally, being human, they are prone to disagree with each other.

All the more striking, then, that there is a certain type of character in a democratic society whose heroism is, in fact, a matter of consensus. It is indeed the firefighter rushing into the Twin Towers on 9/11. It's Lenny Skutnik, the fellow who in 1982 leapt out of his car and jumped into the Potomac River to pull a woman to safety after a plane crash. It's the two young Marines in Iraq who made a split-second decision in the last moments of their lives to open fire on a truck hurtling toward the compound where they were standing guard, thereby preventing the bomb-laden vehicle from entering before it blew up and so saving the lives of their sleeping comrades. It's all those willing to risk their lives to save the lives of others.

Celebrities may think adulation is their due and that special rules apply to them. On the latter point, they may be right. But real heroes of the kind who risk their lives for others do not demand adulation. On the contrary, like my wife's uncle, more often than not they are quick to deny any suggestion that there is anything special about who they are. They specifically disavow any status of superiority as a result of their heroic deeds. As Tina Brown wrote in her preface to *Newsweek*'s "Heroes Issue," " 'Don't call me a hero.' That short sentence—firm, self-effacing, nonnegotiable—ties together all the heroic men and women in this issue. . . . If there is one factor that unites the American heroes we spotlight here . . . it is their adamant refusal to be portrayed as special."

Their reticence in relation to their own exploits is itself a tacit acknowledgment that they understand the greatness of their particular achievement; otherwise, they could talk matter-of-factly about what they had done. But this taciturn self-consciousness is a long way from the towering ambition and inner drive that gave rise to the tragic hero of the classical age—the ultimately unsatisfiable desire to rise above the human.

Contrary to the exhortation of Thomas Carlyle, we don't "bow down" to our heroes. But in our egalitarian way, we can and do recognize our saving heroes in a fashion that actually does evoke Carlyle's "everlasting adamant" to honor achievement: We award them medals and keys to the city. We give them a round of applause. We buy them a beer.

CHAPTER 9

# SACRIFICE AND GENEROSITY

*Making a difference in the lives of others.*
*Teachers, mentors. One night in Wroclaw.*
*Friendship and love.*

When you ask people who their heroes are, you often hear them mention a teacher or a coach or a minister—a mentor who took the trouble to have an inspiring effect on a person at a formative point in their lives. The common theme of heroism in this sense is generosity, someone doing something for you that you perceive as above and beyond the call of duty or the basic requirements of the relationship.

There is an obvious sense in which some of the activities we have discussed in the previous chapter count as acts of generosity, in some cases supreme acts of generosity. A person in trouble in the water, at risk of drowning, has no *right* to be saved by a lifeguard or a passerby. Nor is it easy to make a convincing argument that a passerby has a *duty* to leap into the water. The Potomac River several miles upstream from downtown Washington DC has no lifeguards because it is unsafe under any circumstances to swim there due to the speed of the current. People have been known to fall in, however, and rescuers have jumped in after them. Some would-be rescuers have perished in the attempt. Closer to town, nothing but something within himself *compelled* Lenny Skutnik to jump into the river to aid victims of a plane crash.

The lifeguard is a more complicated case: There actually is a legal responsibility on the part of someone working as a lifeguard to attempt a rescue. But the presumption underlying this duty is that it's generally safe to do so. The activity of rescuing a drowning person is not risk free, of course. Someone flailing in the water in the early stage of drowning, panicked and pumped full of adrenaline, will sometimes endanger a rescuer in the illusory view that this is the way to safety—by grabbing a lifeguard at the shoulders and seeking to get out of the water by pushing down, for example. Even here, however, professional lifeguards are practiced in the moves necessary to get free and continue the rescue. And it is simply not an obligation for them to die trying, though some have. In any case the choice to become a lifeguard entails voluntary assumption of additional risk.

Nor do you have a right to be saved from a burning building. The firefighters and other first responders will do their best, but they likewise are not obliged to die trying to save you. All their training teaches them to be mindful of the risk to themselves and carefully weigh conditions before they decide to enter through the flames. Sometimes, however, they choose to ignore their training and cope with the risk on the fly, as best they can. It worked out for Ptl. Robins, but in some cases, including the spectacular case of 9/11, it did not.

As we have seen in the previous chapter, the sensibility common among modern life-saving heroes tends to downplay if not to forswear the heroic character of the action: All in a day's work. Yet from the point of view of the person saved, it would be churlish in the extreme to take the view that the person doing the saving was just doing a job. Indeed, examples of such churlishness are exceedingly hard to come by. On the end of the person saved, the response is typically overwhelming gratitude. And while elementary politeness in daily life often includes expressions of gratitude to people doing their jobs, typically it is not bare compliance with a job description that calls forth the "thanks," but the decent or better humor of the person doing it. The default setting for a "thank you" may require little more than a neutral demeanor in the performance of a service. But one does not thank a surly shopkeeper except ironically.

So people who have found themselves in the position of having their lives saved typically see generosity in the activity of the person who saved them. They perceive themselves to have been granted a boon that was not their due, theirs by right. They often speak in religious terms: they say they have been "blessed," they talk about a lifesaver as a "guardian angel." Sometimes they attribute their rescue to the action of God or a higher power working through the lifesaver.

But most people don't need to have their lives saved. There are exceptions, of course, starting with the categories of accident, crime, warfare, and serious illness. But none is commonplace in the modern world—at least not until later in life, when the prospect of illness looms larger. Those unlucky enough to experience a brush with death but lucky enough to get past it are often demonstratively grateful to the doctors and others who helped them through it. But those with a need for a lifesaving hero, let alone a life-risking hero, are not present among us in large numbers.

Nevertheless, most people probably have had the experience of what they regard as extraordinary generosity on the part of others in a time of need. I think this experience of the generosity of others connects with the life-risking, lifesaving hero. Although one's benefactor in such cases acts not at the risk of her life, and though her actions aren't necessarily responsible for "saving" you except possibly in some metaphorical sense, her conduct toward you is somehow above and beyond the call of duty.

In what does duty consist? Well, teachers ought to have their lesson plans and coaches of youth teams a command of the sport superior to that of their young charges. Already, this is not always the case. Professional competence doesn't sound like too much to ask for, but it is not infrequently more than one gets.

Nonprofessional social settings can also involve minimum standards of obligation. When you hear about a personal difficulty a friend or acquaintance of yours is experiencing, if you are like most people you will probably say (or text or email) something along the following lines: "If there's anything I can do, let me know." The offer is formal in character; you haven't put anything specific on the table. Of course, unless you are a complete heel, if your acquaintance follows up with a specific request, you'll make good on it. Bring your kid's teammate home from a soccer game when mom is laid up? Of course. Come by and water the plants while your friend is away? No problem.

It's probably fair to say that the deeper the acquaintance, the more that can reasonably be asked, but that the "ask" will be tailored to the particular contours of the relationship. Maybe you have somebody whose dog gets along well with your dog, and you can drop yours off on the way out of town for a couple days. That may or may not be the same person you ask for a ride to the nearest airport, 50 miles from your home.

I am focused here on circumstances of adversity. Of course many people have friends with whom they routinely exchange not only affection but also services, and in which the mutual favors are an important part of the friendship. Couples likewise find advantage in dividing up activities of mutual benefit in accordance with a principle of who is best at what, or who most enjoys or least detests what—from cooking versus washing the dishes, to the venerable honey-do list. The interaction of their individual desires shapes a mutual sense of what is good for the two of them that is greater than the sum of what is good for each of them.

Relations of love and friendship between two people generally reflect some kind of equilibrium in terms of the expectations each has for the other. Of course the balance is subject to modification based on the will of the parties. I think most of us at one time or another have run across or heard tell of characters who ask too much and offer too little in return. We have also probably seen cases in which the existing equilibrium between two people seems out of whack, perhaps even dangerously and exploitatively so. Under those circumstances, perhaps an intervention from a third party to address the unhealthy codependence would be a good idea. In any case, the life of an individual bereft of love and friendship is, for most of us, a horrible thing to contemplate.

Perhaps a small fraction of us are so blessed or so fortunate as never to run into a personal difficulty. But not most of us. Never having been tortured by the Medicis, I will never claim to have endured the "many hardships and dangers" Machiavelli says he experienced in coming to understand the world. But rather recently and not for the first time, I found myself in a difficult spot being treated with a generosity to which I had no right and which I did not expect.

So with your indulgence, a personal story. I was in Wroclaw, Poland, attending an international conference. Earlier that day, I had met up with an old acquaintance from Berlin, U., whom I hadn't seen in several years. We talked for half an hour or so and thought we might sit together at dinner that evening to continue the conversation.

As it happened, the dinner featured table assignments for the guests, and we weren't at the same one. Our paths didn't recross until later that night, as we were getting on the bus for the 15-minute ride from the dinner venue back to the conference hotel. Even so, we couldn't sit together. U. got on the bus as it was nearly filled, and the place beside me was already occupied. We were able to do no more than "hello" each other as she got on.

Back in front of the hotel, as I was approaching the door of the bus to get off, I saw that U. was waiting. This pleased me. *Not too late for a drink at the bar*, I was thinking—as my right leg missed the last of the steps on the way out of the bus. I came down badly, my leg buckled, and I landed on the ground. U., along with another acquaintance I'd made at the conference, rushed over and helped me up, urgently asking if I was okay. I was embarrassed, of course. I told them my knee had given out, but that I wasn't in any pain (an ill-founded conclusion based on shock and adrenaline, turns out), and when they asked if I could walk, I said I thought so. I took a step—and promptly went down again.

Embarrassment blended seamlessly into mortification as they hauled me up once more, this time not letting go, U. on the left, J. on the right. Their arms around my shoulders and mine around theirs, we conducted a five-legged shamble into the hotel lobby, my right leg essentially along for the ride. They eased me down onto the banquette, and talk quickly turned to an ambulance and the emergency room. I agreed they were a good idea. J. went off in search of some ice for my knee. U. sat on the banquette next to me to wait for the EMTs.

Was it really true that before getting on the transatlantic leg of the flight to Wroclaw, I had been musing about the inevitability of something bad happening on one of my trips one of these days? Yes, it was. This was because of my generally good luck with travel. Apart from an occasional bag going astray, my worst piece of misfortune so far dated to a trip twenty years before, and the sum of my bad luck was missing an essential connection in Frankfurt, therefore necessitating the abandonment of the trip and turning around to catch the next flight home. It was certainly a waste of time, but back then booze was still free in coach. Not a great hardship.

Jinx? Did I talk myself into tripping off a bus to for the purpose of vindicating my foreboding? I don't think so. No, I think I was simply failing to think about stepping off the bus safely when I was stepping off the bus. In youth, it's a mistake you probably get away with. After 50, you should pay closer attention.

Back on the banquette, it was dawning on me that I was about to undergo a bit of an ordeal. That there are worse such, I readily concede. Wroclaw is now a modern city in a modern Western country, one for which I have long felt great affection. It's not like I had to rush into a burning building to rescue someone. It wasn't even likely to entail an encounter with, shall we say, premodern medicine. Nevertheless, my leg was an uncertain magnitude of screwed up, I don't speak Polish, I didn't know where they would be taking me or how long I would be at the hospital, I was going there in an ambulance but getting back afterward was an unknown. I had the princely sum of 150 zlotys in my wallet (a little less than $50), the charge in my phone was down to about 20 percent, and I had a panel to appear on the next day and then a tight window to get to the airport for my flight out of Poland. Assuming I could fly. What are the rules for flying with a badly abused leg? One need not wallow in self-pity, but yes, it was going to be a hard night.

U., who is delightfully talkative, then said matter-of-factly that she would come with me to the hospital. And so we arrive at the point of this story.

I found her declaration—it wasn't really an offer so much as a statement of fact—simply startling. I could see somebody wanting to keep me company in the hotel lobby waiting for the ambulance to arrive. That was very kind of her. But by now, it was nearing midnight, and, well, really? Come along to the hospital? For God knows how long? In the middle of the night? I protested. To no avail. U. said she had been looking forward to having a drink with me, so instead, she'd come along. Although U. is altogether a singular individual, one could be forgiven for taking her comment as a flawless expression of the logic of Teutonic *Gemütlichkeit*.

I found myself cheering up a little, a sentiment that abated briefly when the EMTs said U. wasn't allowed to ride along in the ambulance, but revived when U. insisted she would take a cab. As my gurney was getting strapped into the ambulance, I decided I had better also let the relevant conference folks know what was going on—especially before my phone went dead. I dashed off a quick typo-ridden email to my old friend and collaborator L., a conference VIP who was chairing the panel I was scheduled to appear on the next morning, copying as well my host at the sponsoring organization. At my request, one of the EMT guys typed the name of the hospital we were heading to into the e-mail.

L. e-mailed me right back, asking for my phone number, and called at once. He said he would come straightaway to the hospital. I tried to demur, noting that I would be fine and anyway U. was on her way. He would have none of this. To silence my objection, he demanded to know if U. spoke Polish, which she doesn't. L. does. I admitted as much. So it was that L., too, arrived at the hospital, having taken time first to get hold of and bring in tow the young Polish graduate student-volunteer assigned to see to his needs at the conference. I was at the hospital with U. about an hour before they arrived. I don't have a clear recollection of much of what we talked about, but I don't think the content of the conversation mattered nearly as much as having someone to talk to.

With L. and his aide-de-camp M. on the scene, after a while U. felt comfortable saying goodnight, maybe around 1:30 in the morning. L. and M. made it unmistakably clear that they would be with me for the duration, and so they were, conferring with nurses and doctors, checking on my comfort, wheeling me to the door of the men's room, and finally bundling me and my doctor-immobilized leg into a cab upon being discharged at around 3:30 a.m. They rode with me back to the hotel, and then provided the shoulders to lean on that got me back into my room. L. put M. in charge of overseeing early the next morning the acquisition of the items the doctors had ordered for me—a leg immobilizer, crutches, and a blood thinner for the plane ride back, which was prophylaxis against the risk of a blood clot at altitude. I would miss the panel, but make the flight for home as scheduled, as safe and sound as circumstances permitted.

I won't say that by the time I was back in my hotel room my mental state was fine. I will say that it was infinitely better than it could possibly have been in the absence of the involvement of U., L., and M. The sheer magnitude of their benefaction in response to my troubles seemed to me to be awe-inspiring. It still does.

I am just guessing, but my guess is that such acts of personal generosity, above and beyond the call of duty as perceived by their beneficiaries, are countless every day. When people casually call out "my hero!" in response to an expectation exceeded or a difficult challenge successfully met, it's this "above and beyond the call" element to which they refer.

Does that make U., L., and M. my heroes? It is not difficult to philosophize oneself into a state of curmudgeonly dudgeon over a supposed falling-off in the meaning of the term "hero" when it is routinely applied to the likes of your high school freshman English teacher or your little league coach or somebody who stayed up late with you one night.

From Achilles to—fill in a name. And indeed, there are variations on this theme that cannot but seem a bit preposterous: Odysseus had a rough time getting home after the Trojan War; the evening rush hour traffic is a bitch; therefore, commuters are heroes.

But it's worth our time to consider more fully what's going on when people evoke personal heroes, somebody who meant something special to them. Because when people say they have heroes these days, that's usually the type of individual they are talking about.

In the early 1990s, the Drexel University sociologist David V. Porpora conducted survey research in Philadelphia asking people whether they personally had heroes and, if so, who they might be. He then classified their responses into five categories (plus "other"): celebrities, political heroes, religious heroes, arts heroes (including scientists), and what he called "local heroes," defined as "heroes of ordinary life who are acquaintances of the respondent." Mentions of parents, teachers, clergy, and friends were classified as local heroes.

Porpora found that most respondents did not say they had a hero or heroes. Around 40 percent said they did. Among that 40 percent, the most prominently mentioned by far were local heroes, at 47.2 percent, followed by political heroes (28.8 percent), celebrities (15.6 percent), and religious (14 percent).

But what about our much-vaunted, media-driven celebrity culture, which we discussed in Chapter 7? Porpora conducted his survey in the waning days of mass culture, before its fragmentation into wikiculture. Mass media then were certainly in the business of visiting fame and fortune upon a select few. Porpora's survey results indicate that whatever it is the media may have been selling, people weren't necessarily buying, at least not in large numbers and certainly therefore not as an inevitable outcome of heavy media attention and hype. To the contrary: The local heroes people mention most frequently have presumably received little to no media attention for what they have done. There is a touching genuineness to respondents to Porpora's survey citing people know one knows or has heard of.

The assertions respondents made were entirely a product of their own judgment. No one told them to favor a parent or teacher or close friend when sociologists start calling on the telephone; nor would those whom respondents cited ever know from the survey research that they had been favored in such a fashion. It's hard to see any undue influence as a possibility in respondents' judgments, nor the possibility of ulterior motive. Local heroes just happen to be the heroic type that people come up with most often when they think about their own lives.

Once the life-risking hero comes to embody not unquenchable personal ambition or an inner sense of superiority over others, but a willingness to do something *for* others, even for a stranger, then we have opened the door to a stairway of generosity. Its first step is the smallest unnecessary kindness, and it leads up from there to increasing heights of beneficence under increasing difficulty to the top step, the entry door to a modern Valhalla, for the hero who gives her life to save another. Beyond that door, you will find the 9/11 firefighters who perished and the Congressional Medal of Honor winners who covered grenades. I like to think of Ptl. Robins in the rotation of those pulling shifts as sentry. To describe as "heroes" those occupying a place on the stairs somewhere below the top, as people often do, is no degeneration of the idea of heroism, but an indication of the high value we attach to generosity in the modern world.

Why? Because generosity fills a void. The modern world is grounded in the idea of individual right and reciprocal obligation. If I have the right to do something, and you prevent me from doing it, you have violated my rights, and I can look to the institutions of government to take action to annul your violation. At least symbolically, the system restores to me what you took away. When rights belong to all people—not just the king (as in the "divine right" thereof) or to a hereditary noble class of property owners—then political order has managed to travel about as far as it can from its origin in the untrammeled rule of the strong. We should value modern political order highly. Though it is a collective or social political achievement, rather than the handiwork of a single human being, it is worthy of comparison with political achievement on the heroic scale of Julius Caesar.

Although modern political order points to and protects the legitimacy of all human desires that do not impinge on the rights of others, it offers no guidance for choosing among legitimate desires. To many critics, this has long been the top entry on the rap sheet on classical liberalism. If securing the freedom to "follow your bliss," in the words of Joseph Campbell, is the ultimate goal of politics, then politics seems to have nothing to say about good or bad (or just better or worse) forms of bliss to pursue. "Consenting adults" is more or less the last word. Put formally, the only rule is a metarule, actually a negative version of the Golden Rule: Don't treat others in a way you would not want to be treated yourself. Certain actions are punishable by law; others, such as shouting abuse at strangers in the street, are protected by law as "free speech" but prohibited by social sanction. Refraining from treating others as you would not wish to be treated is good advice, but it's not a lot to go on in figuring out how you should live.

Modern political order is thus no more able to provide the *satisfaction* of all legitimate human desires than any other form of political order. At best, the modern world fulfills a precondition for such satisfaction by getting political authorities out of the way of your pursuit of what you reasonably want and into the business of enforcing your right to pursue it when others wrongly step on you. But there are limits to how much the state can do for you. If you need a friend, or someone to love and love you back, you cannot turn to the political world and demand that one be issued to you. I submit that people in general do need friends and others to love and love them back. Which is to say, they feel a need for the generosity and care of others—by no means all others, but at least *some*—and on their good days they feel a sense of satisfaction in being generous to someone else.

This impulse seems as old as the first humans, if not indeed older. If one element in the emergence of "the animal that talks" is the assertion of power, as we speculated in Chapter 1, another is the expression of caring. Power compels; caring aggregates two or more people voluntarily. I note, without expertise, that evolutionary biologists have become very interested in the question of where regard for others comes from. The philosophical leanings of the modern world have tended to seek the answer to this question by returning to the individual posing it and inquiring there, as if others were simply a mirror in which we are better able to see ourselves. All roads lead back to self-aggrandizement, or Nietzsche's will to power. Caring about others is an epiphenomenon—a triviality of sentiment, or perhaps an illusion in a world shaped ultimately by power.

Yet the expression of power in the form of political order has changed over the millennia, whereas the caring will does not appear to have changed at all. If anything, people seem to have expanded the scope of those about whom they care, to include in some instances people they have never met. Hence the outpouring of generosity from denizens of the modern world from time to time in response to natural disasters and political catastrophes. People seem also to be able to increase the reach of their care for others without necessarily diminishing the strength of their commitment to those about whom they care most. Achilles cared about Patroclus as no other, and Patroclus Achilles. But Patroclus cared about the fate of the Greeks as well, a care that Achilles, "great in his greatness," could never muster.

Among the things that power compels is attention. Hence the stories of the powerful from time immemorial. Hence tales of heroes in the classical mold. Some saving-style heroes have garnered attention on the same scale. But an act of generosity need not be supremely sacrificial nor even widely acknowledged to count as heroic to the person who is its recipient. That's what personal or local heroes are all about. We often refer to such persons collectively as "unsung heroes." They are the reminders on a scale appropriate to our political order that generosity—including love, friendship, and the caring will—is something without which human life would be incomplete.

## CHAPTER 10

# THE RETURN OF THE SLAYING HERO?

*Scenarios all too imaginable.*
*The resources of the modern world in combating the*
*return of the slaying hero.*
*The success of the modern world as a project of*
*permanent vigilance.*

Thus we have the hero's progress from the very beginning of history down to our own time, the striking evolution of the meaning of human greatness from its origin in epic self-striving in response to an inner sense of greatness to its modern, democratic incarnation as the willingness to risk your life to save someone else's. From slaying to saving—from the highest, riskiest expression of self-regard to the highest, riskiest expression of generosity and the caring will.

And if that were the end of the matter, we, the unheroic—unheroic certainly in the classical sense and for most of us, in the modern sense as well—might simply call it a day. We enjoy a measure of peace and personal security unknown to mankind before modern times. Instead of preparing mentally and physically for the inevitable recurrence of times of strife, we can take to our couches and busy ourselves with the enjoyment of the leisure time the modern world generously allows us.

We can watch tales of the heroic on television, play Wii games in which we reimagine ourselves as heroes, and catch up on the foibles of the rich and famous, those reassuring reminders that nowadays fame comes warts and all, or not at all. In our better moments, we are probably even willing to get off the couch and spend some time cultivating the less risky forms of generosity on which the modern world also depends: coaching Little League, being a mentor, doing a favor for a friend in need.

Unfortunately, that's not where matters end. We still have a few loose ends to tie up. And, not to put too fine a point on it, the stakes are high—something like the survival of the modern world itself and the egalitarian ethos that underpins it. We may be done with the slaying hero. But the slaying hero may not be done with us.

We have already met a great many problematic historical characters in the course of our survey, and we have by turns seen how the modern world has surmounted them. Achilles has no place here. Even the Romans thought, in the end, that Julius Caesar was a bit much, and no American general would think to order his army to cross the Rubicon—the Potomac?—to overthrow the republic and install himself as emperor. Alexander's copy of the *Iliad* would lie under his pillow in the insane asylum. Joan of Arc in the U.S. military? Don't ask, don't tell. Napoleon at least brought the Napoleonic code and those newfangled "rights of man," the democratic spirit, along with him, partly mitigating (at least for some) the concern that he was trying to conquer the world just for his own sake.

The modern world is, in short, very good at weeding out and breeding out those of a classically heroic bent who might seek to impose the old slaying ways in service to their personal sense of self. This is good news for the egalitarian ethos, and for the aforementioned peace and personal security of its adherents. But two large problems loom. The first is the potential for a serious outside challenge to the modern world and its ethos. The second, more subtle, is the potential vulnerability of the modern world to internal disintegration.

To restate the first problem more baldly: What if an old-school slaying hero decides to conquer the world, that is, our world—to conquer and subjugate *us*? Do we, generous in spirit and reluctant to slay as we are, have the capacity and will to resist? Would we even recognize the threat as it gathered?

And the second: What if our egalitarian ethos contains the seeds of its own destruction? Could illiberal internal forces use the doctrines and practices of freedom and equality to further a hidden agenda asserting their own claim of superiority? And if so, again, would we see it coming in time to act?

I wish these questions were merely hypothetical or theoretical. Unfortunately, they are not. In fact, they are frighteningly well-grounded historically. Before the collapse of Soviet communism gave impetus to the "end of History" vogue first popularized by Francis Fukuyama and still propounded without direct acknowledgment but with minimal alteration by the seers of globalization, the regnant impression among serious twentieth-century thinkers ran quite the opposite direction: Far from pointing to the inevitability of progress, defined as the spread of liberal, democratic, capitalism—for our purposes, the modern world—the ghastly historical record of the twentieth century was mainly seen to constitute precedent for human-caused death and destruction on an ever more massive scale. The human propensity for assertion of claims of superiority and the seeking of exactions from the weaker, combined with the progress of technology and its capacity to kill people in exponentially increasing numbers, could best be understood as the precursors of Armageddon.

No one these days calls Hitler a "hero." In Germany, it's even against the law. On the contrary, we have different appellations for Hitler, beginning with "villain." We need that word "villain" very urgently, to point out that there are event-making individuals of whom we emphatically do not approve. In the age of classical heroism, by contrast, the many slain were not an especially important part of the story. At the time, no one was especially disturbed when Crassus, fresh from putting down Spartacus's slave rebellion, crucified one of his captives every few hundred yards on the way back to Rome, some 6,000 slave rebels in all. Or rather, witnesses were likely terribly disturbed, above all by the involuntary sense of awe they felt for someone capable of such a deed. Of such deeds Roman heroes were made.

Hitler needs a different sobriquet because we do care about 6 million Jews, as well as the millions of others who died in the war he demanded. But he was a hero to many Germans at the time, and not just the unsophisticated and ignorant. Not least in love with the führer was one of the greatest thinkers of the twentieth century, Martin Heidegger, who interpreted the "motorization of the Wehrmacht" as a "metaphysical act" whereby the "inner truth and greatness" of National Socialism would assert itself decisively in battle over the wimpy, individualist, egalitarian metaphysics of the bourgeois, democratic, capitalist world. Heidegger was wrong on the outcome and presumably, therefore, wrong on the metaphysics. But it did take all of the time, effort, blood, and treasure known as World War II to make the point that the modern world has no place for Hitlers in it.

Moreover, about the Germans: They considered themselves, in the late nineteenth and early twentieth century, a highly civilized people, not without justification: the land of Goethe and Beethoven and such. Given the givens, Germany was not such a bad place for Jews to live until it became an impossible place for Jews to live. There was, of course, a certain backdrop of anti-Semitism. But the general consensus among scholars seems to be: no Hitler, no Holocaust. The big problem with the Weimar republic established after the wreckage of World War I was not that social conditions somehow pointed inevitably to the Final Solution; it was that liberal Weimar was too weak politically to prevent the rise of Hitler.

The "modern world" of which we have been speaking does not exhibit anything like the fragility of the Weimar republic, nor is an army likely to gather and roll over us any time soon. The United States indisputably—and many of its allies, though some to a lesser degree—knows how to fight. But knowing how to fight is not the same as knowing *when* to fight. Political leaders make such decisions, and unless we can assure ourselves that they will never again fall prey to the wishful thinking and making-the-best-of-things that led Neville Chamberlain to pursue a policy of appeasement toward Hitler, then a genuine risk remains.

As well, there is the distinct possibility that the danger is a modern world that ends not with a bang but a whimper. It would take the form of the gradual abandonment of the classically liberal principles that animate the modern world and provide its dynamism.

What would such a decline and fall look like? Again, the question is not entirely hypothetical. We have had a fairly robust and at times bitter debate in the United States, and in the modern world more broadly, over free speech and the limits of what is sayable. One can indeed point to some constriction of the realm of the permissible, in the form of so-called "political correctness" (though it must surely be viewed in the context of the vast increase in other areas of permissibility, for example in almost everything having to do with sex). This debate is instructive because it illustrates how ethical imperatives collide, how the contest is not between good and bad but between contending ideas of what's good. "Hate speech" is not good and can indeed inflame, though suppressing it may be worse than letting it go. Where to draw the line? The problem is that reasonable people do, in fact, differ, and that unreasonable people may be willing to exploit this disagreement for their own ends.

So far, we have mainly had a debate about speech, and in the United States at least (less so in Europe), free speech is still winning even at its most controversial. But there's worse on the a la carte menu of potential decline, and it may similarly take the form of competing ideas of what's good. What would be the psychological effect of a gradual, seemingly inexorable increase in crime of all kinds, such that people no longer felt comfortable on the streets of cities, towns, and suburbs, with whole neighborhoods left to fend for themselves, unvisited by the police or the law the police stand for? People would not like it, but what would they do about it? Would they impose a crackdown, perhaps martial law, to get matters under control? Or would that be deemed too extreme? Would those with means retreat into ever-smaller enclaves and leave the rest of the country to a new Hobbesian state of nature? What kind of "modern world" would that be?

Perhaps the context for such a development would be long-term economic stagnation resistant to the best efforts of policymakers. The American political system is designed to act slowly, which is a protection against one form of risk. But suppose political paralysis becomes endemic and resists all efforts at compromise, or suppose the contending rescue plans are based on premises so different that they really cannot be reconciled. What if the American dream really does collapse: a "land of opportunity" no more. Will the have-nots be content to remain on the bottom, or will they find ways to assert their grievances?

Perhaps a well-conducted homegrown terrorist campaign could permanently close the public square. Perhaps travel abroad could become too dangerous, either because the transportation infrastructure becomes untrustworthy due to advances in terrorist methods or because what Kant called the "cosmopolitan right," the freedom to walk the streets in security in someone else's country, falls into abeyance as people worldwide start pointing fingers and guns.

And perhaps we might see, after all, the emergence of some charismatic character offering relief from all of the above—though at a price. Say, your civil liberties and your democracy. And perhaps a beaten-down people would be willing to pay that price. And perhaps the leader would get results, at least in the beginning, and the people would celebrate him or her as a hero—a saving hero. Our hero would likely be content to be judged as such, not least because it affords the kind of legitimacy that allows one to get away with more of what one wants to do, including rolling up the political opposition and crushing dissent.

We wouldn't call our leader "The Leader," of course: too much bad karma from the twentieth century. But the result could be much the same, and as long as our leader refrained from killing 6 million more Jews, any comparison to Hitler would be out of bounds, and rightly so. (An additional problem for the modern world is that once Hitler has set your standard for villainy, it becomes all the more difficult to call out his epigones for malevolence that is, almost necessarily, on a smaller scale.)

Inaction in the face of threats from abroad or from internal subversion is unfortunately not the only way things can go wrong in the age of the saving hero. There is also the risk of *too-hasty* action from political leaders. Perhaps a threat from abroad is exaggerated and the result is an overreaction whose unforeseen consequences turn out to be crippling. Fortunately, though its costs in lives and dollars were high, the Iraq war did not cripple the United States. But who knows about the next war? And what an acute problem of leadership it is to face the fact that one may not know in advance whether one is overreacting to, properly responding to, or underestimating danger. Disaster is a possible outcome for the cautious as well as the rash.

There is an obvious analogy on the domestic scene. I am relatively untroubled by the surveillance provisions of the Patriot Act. But I am not troubled that others are troubled. We need constant vigilance to ensure that *necessary* government encroachment on civil liberties doesn't slide into unnecessary encroachment merely *desirable* from the government's point of view. At the same time, we will also be in trouble if our resistance to infringement of civil liberties excessively impinges our ability to be vigilant.

A final problem arises at the highest level: The modern world has universal aspirations; it claims to know what rights people should enjoy everywhere, hence the Universal Declaration of Human Rights, which was perhaps the United Nations' finest hour in articulation of the norms by which we wish to live (even if many of the nations that signed on to the Universal Declaration were insincere and had no intention of living up to its principles). It is indisputably a good thing to help others realize their aspirations to live according to the principles of the Universal Declaration, and to do what one can to encourage other states to respect the rights of their people—at a minimum, to refrain from killing them on a large scale.

But the modern world is not an innocent babe. It has power at its disposal, indeed, vast power. Power so great that leaders might from time to time find themselves tempted to use it to try to hasten the rest of the world along on its course to modernity. Here lies not only the risk that the rest of the world will not transform so readily, but also the danger of political leadership that begins slaying in the name of saving. Once the U.S. government decided to topple Saddam Hussein, the leaders of the occupying power felt they owed the Iraqi people a sincere effort to try to set up a rights-regarding, democratic, liberal-leaning political system. The difficulty of doing so, with the total dead numbering well over 100,000 by the time the United States military departed from Iraq in 2011, ought to remind us that the desire to set up a rights-regarding, democratic, liberal-leaning political system is a woefully insufficient reason to go around toppling governments. All the more so in light of the swift descent of Iraq into chaos in the absence of an ongoing U.S. presence.

The "saving hero" is a figure fully compatible with the modern world and its egalitarian first principle, and indeed a necessary figure for that world as heroism takes the form of sacrifice of self and generosity toward others—the caring will. The modern world would be self-contradictory and unintelligible with an ethos that said, in 2010: Those 33 miners trapped underground in Chile are probably dead, so what's the point of a big rescue operation? Or, on the battlefield: When the going gets rough, leave the wounded behind and live to fight another day—or maybe shoot the wounded to put them out of their misery.

But as in all cases, the human capacity for speech and reason enables us not only to say what is and to reason and speculate together, but also to call something what it is not. "Democratic Kampuchea" was the name the Khmer Rouge gave to Cambodia when they came to power in 1974. The state's new name did not quite capture what the Khmer

Rouge leadership had in mind for the country, namely, a totalitarian state undertaking class-based genocide against its own people.

The figure of the "saving hero" is no less subject to distortion into its opposite. Osama bin Laden may have been content to see himself as an old-fashioned "slaying hero," cackling in glee as he heard tell of the towers falling. Perhaps the single most memorable slogan on the terrorist side of the "war on terror," or whatever one wishes to call it (if anything), is: "We love death more than you love life." So take that, cowards.

But bin Laden also cast himself as trying to save Islam from the infidels, heretics, and apostates. Apparently, in his final years, he also took an interest in climate change, excoriating the modern world for its environmental destructiveness. Notwithstanding the widespread desire for collective action to combat climate change, the notion of bin Laden as savior of the environment was one most of the modern world could resist. But one could not fairly accuse bin Laden of inconsistency in the means and ends he advocated: If, per his initiative, political and social conditions worldwide transformed into those of Afghanistan under the pious Taliban in September 2001, one result would certainly be a substantial reduction in carbon emissions.

It is obviously perverse or worse to view bin Laden as a "saving hero." But that is no proof against a more subtle attempt by a slaying hero to pass as a saving hero, the better to serve villainous ambition. On a small scale, we see such lesser forms of villainy all too often, these days often caught on tape: for example, those LA police officers venting their racist view of citizens they are supposed to serve and protect. Villainy usually flies a false flag. We, the unvillainous (to our credit, we are not merely unheroic), like to say that's because villains are "ashamed" to show their true colors. Maybe. But maybe they aren't the least bit ashamed and fly a false flag because that's how they can best get their way. We should at least consider the possibility that a villain acts utterly without remorse, because if we don't, we may not understand villainy well enough to appreciate just how dangerous a villain can be.

So it turns out the modern world is not quite as foolproof safe against the return of the slaying hero as we might like to think. The radical challenge to political order a slaying hero represents is not something the modern world has eliminated from the realm of possibility but merely holds in abeyance.

The resources to continue to do so, the modern world generates in abundance. The states and societies comprising the modern world, full of people who think in the category of others "like themselves," are economically prosperous and expend significant resources on their own defense against external threat. Their social models are subject to objection and criticism from within on the grounds that they have failed in one way or another to fulfill the promises of an egalitarian and democratic age. But the criticism, even when radical, does not leave the horizon of classical liberalism and egalitarianism. No one calls for the return of aristocracy or of a king with absolute power.

Tocqueville worried, with reason, about whether the march of "equality of conditions" would lead people gradually to abandon the desire to have liberty or freedom along with equality (661–665). The result might be a kind of democratic centralism, a superstate in which every little boy or girl could aspire to become general secretary or supreme leader, on one hand, but in the alternative would also accept—per Ernst Jünger, perhaps even relish—a role as cannon fodder when necessary.

The good news is that illiberal or unfree equality seems to offer insufficient satisfaction to the people living under its principles to constitute a stable solution to the age-old problems of politics. From the aspiring totalitarianism of the Soviet Union and Maoist China to modern-day theocracies in the mold of Revolutionary Iran or aspirational al Qaeda, something is missing, and it isn't really equality (though as an empirical matter, per George Orwell in *Animal Farm*, "all animals are equal, but some are more equal than others"). Democratic centralism, or unfree egalitarianism, looks for but hasn't located a substitute for the saving hero and the related caring will that thrive best under conditions of freedom. Of course, under such regimes as well as under liberal democratic governance, the modern saving hero can indeed surface and generosity above and beyond the call of duty does indeed take place. Though individually embodied to varying degrees, the caring will is primal and universal. But in the case of unfree political order, such personal generosity and sacrifice exist in contrast to rather than in harmony with it.

Nor, finally, is it obvious that would-be terrorists such as Adis Medunjanin, now serving a life sentence for plotting a suicide bomb attack on the New York City subway, are right in the implications they draw from their famous declaration. Medunjanin, on the eve of his capture, spoke the familiar words to a 911 operator, "We love death more than you love life." Even though the statement is likely true, it by no means follows that those who "love death" are inevitably stronger and destined to prevail in a struggle against those who "love life." If the love of life meant a universal unwillingness among lovers of life to risk death under any circumstances, then Medunjanin and those like him might be on to something. But that is demonstrably not the case. The willingness of some to risk their lives for the sake of others, on the battlefield or in a burning building, may in fact be a more powerful tool at the disposal of the principles it defends than love of death in support of different principles.

The empirical test of this hypothesis is the ongoing ability of the modern world to prevent the slaying hero from coming back.

# ACKNOWLEDGMENTS

I worked on this book under the auspices of the Hoover Institution's Boyd and Jill Smith Task Force on the Virtues of a Free Society. Thanks to my colleagues on the task force: Peter Berkowitz and David Brady, the co-chairs; and Gerard Bradley, James W. Ceasar, William Damon, Harvey C. Mansfield, Russell Muirhead, Clifford Orwin, and Diana Schaub. Thanks to Hoover and its Director, John Raisian, for support for this work in particular and for general support for me as a research fellow.

Thanks to Richard Starr at the *Weekly Standard*, John Podhoretz and his predecessors Neal Kozodoy and Norman Podhoretz at *Commentary*, and Mary Eberstadt, then my colleague at *Policy Review*, for their excellent contributions as editors of previous versions of arguments here. Thanks also to Susan Arellano at Templeton Press for good advice on the project.

Thanks once again to Bill Damon, and to Henrik Bering, Bruce Jackson, Lee Harris, Craig Kennedy, Jim Mattis, and Kori Schake for reading and commenting on the draft manuscript.

Thanks to Ben Atlas and Teresa Lewi for research assistance.

Thanks to Lynn Chu and Glenn Hartley, my agents, and Roger Kimball and his staff at Encounter.

Thanks to my wife, Tina Lindberg, and my daughters, Abby and Molly, for being exactly who they are.

# SOURCES AND REFERENCES

## CHAPTER 1. GODS AND HEROES

"*zoon logon echon*"—Apparently no one can find exactly that phrase in Aristotle. In his *Nicomachean Ethics*, he uses *tou logon echontos* to describe the distinguishing feature of human beings. See Hans Georg Gadamer, *Praise of Theory* (Yale University Press, 1988), 145 n. 11. Martin Heidegger wrote about the singular importance of recovering the original meaning of *zoon logon echon* at some length. Martin Heidegger, *Being and Time*, Joan Stambaugh, trans. (State University of New York Press, 1996), Sections 6 and 7.

"the multiplicity of languages"—The story of the tower of Babel (Genesis 11:4-9) has many parallels in other traditions. See James George Frazer, *Folklore in the Old Testament: Studies in Comparative Religion, Legend and Law* (Macmillan, 1923), 143-152.

"Tarzan, Mowgli"—Edgar Rice Burroughs, *Tarzan of the Apes & Other Tales* (Gollancz, Centenary Edition, 2012); Rudyard Kipling, *The Jungle Book* (Macmillan, 1894).

"Danielle Crockett"—Lane Gregory, "The girl in the window," *Tampa Bay Times* (July 31, 2008).

"the origin of language"—Needless to say, scholarly opinion varies considerably. For a discussion of the contending theories, see Maggie Tallerman and Kathleen Rite Gibson, eds., *The Oxford Handbook of Language Evolution* (Oxford

University Press, 2012). My view here places a dual emphasis on language as an assertion of power and on language as the ground of intersubjectivity.

"In the beginning was the Word"—John 1:1. All biblical quotations in this book come from the New American Standard Bible.

"Cicero"—Marcus Tullius Cicero, *Tusculan Disputations,* XXX.

"Montaigne"—Michel de Montaigne, *Essays*, XIX.

"the first cave paintings"—Hélène Valladas, "Direct radiocarbon dating of prehistoric cave paintings by accelerator mass spectrometry," *Measurement Science and Technology* 14 (2003), 1487-1492.

"the state of nature as Thomas Hobbes imagined it"—Thomas Hobbes, *Leviathan*, XIII.

"Krishna"—Barbara Stoler Miller, trans., *The Bhagavad-Gita* (Bantam, 1986), II 47.

"Rousseau"—Jean-Jacques Rousseau, *Discourse on This Question: Which is the Virtue Most Necessary for a Hero . . .* in *The Collected Writings of Rousseau, Volume IV* (University Press of New England, 1994), 10.

"'a victorious rampage . . .'"—Seth L. Schein, *The Mortal Hero: An Introduction to Homer's* Iliad (University of California Press, 1984), 80.

"inner greatness"—See Bernard M.W. Knox, *The Heroic Temper: Studies in Sophoclean Tragedy* (University of California Press, 1964; 1983). Knox's discussion places considerable emphasis on the supposed need of the hero to explain himself to others. It's true that heroes in plays do a lot of talking, in the nature of the art form. But they don't do so because they need the approval of others. They may give voice to their "inner greatness," or the perfection they seek to cultivate in themselves, but their sense of inner greatness does not depend on others.

"*Iliad*"—Unless otherwise noted, I have taken all quotations from the *Iliad* from Robert Fagles's translation: Homer, *The Iliad,* Robert Fagles, trans. (Penguin Books, 1998). The first edition was published by Viking Penguin in 1990. The passages quoted are identified in the text by book and line number in the Fagles translation.

"Eliot"—T.S. Eliot, "Hamlet and His Problems," *The Sacred Wood* (Alfred A. Knopf, 1921).

"homoerotic attachment"—This view of the relationship between Achilles and Patroclus has ancient roots. Phaedrus, a character in Plato's dialogue *The Symposium*, describes Achilles and Patroclus as lovers, and refers to an earlier play by Aeschylus that does the same. *Symposium*, 179e-180a.

"great in his greatness"—The phrase occurs just after Achilles learns of Patroclus's death, as Achilles is in the full initial throes of lamentation, rubbing soot and dirt into his face to disfigure himself in grief. The Greek phrase is *megas megalōsti*. Fagles renders it "Overpowered in all his power" (XVIII, 28), which is beautiful and clever, but misleading. It's not that grief as such has overcome the great man, it's that the grief *of the great man* has led *even* the great man to abase himself. Schein, *Mortal Hero*, 130.

"*Odyssey*"—All quotations are from the Fagles translation. Homer, *The Odyssey*, Robert Fagles, trans. (Penguin Books, 2006). The first edition was published by Viking Penguin in 1996. The passages quoted are identified in the text by book and line number in the Fagles translation.

"Heracles"—See, for example, *Odyssey* XI 711-717.

## CHAPTER 2. THE DANGER OF HEROES

"Melos"—The Melian dialogue in Thucydides, *History of the Peloponnesian War*, XVII.

"*Hiero*"—The translation quoted here is by Marvin Kendrick, revised by Seth Benardette, and appears in Leo Strauss, *On Tyranny*, Victor Gourevitch and Michael S. Roth, eds. (University of Chicago Press, Revised and Expanded Edition, 2000).

"Lucretia"—Titus Livy, *History of Rome*, Rev. Canon Roberts, trans. (E. P. Dutton, 1912). Citations are to chapter numbers in Book I. Dionysius of Halicarnassus, *The Roman Antiquities*, Edward Spelman trans. (Loeb Library Vol. 2, 1939). Citations are to chapter numbers in Book IV. William Shakespeare, *The Rape of Lucrece*, in W.G. Clark and W. Aldis Wright, eds. *Globe Shakespeare* (Grossett & Dunlap, 1864). Citations are to stanza numbers.

"Coriolanus"—Plutarch, *Lives*, *Caius Marcius Coriolanus*, Bernadotte Perrin, ed. (G.P. Putnam's Sons, 1916). Citation is to chapter number. William Shakespeare,

*Coriolanus*, in W.G. Clark and W. Aldis Wright, eds. *Globe Shakespeare* (Grossett & Dunlap, 1864).

"Alcibiades"—Plato, *Alcibiades*, D.S. Hutchinson, trans.; and *Symposium*, Alexander Nehamas and Paul Woodruff, trans.; in C.D.C. Reeve, ed. *Plato on Love* (Hackett, 2006). See also Plutarch, *Lives*, *Alcibiades*, Bernadotte Perrin, trans. (G.P. Putnam's Sons, 1916).

"Julius Caesar"—I have relied on Christian Meier, *Caesar: A Biography* (Basic Books, 1982) and Philip Freeman, *Julius Caesar* (Simon and Schuster, 2008). See also Plutarch, *Lives*, *Caesar*, Bernadotte Perrin, ed. (G.P. Putnam's Sons, 1916); and Suetonius, *The Twelve Caesars*, Robert Graves, trans., revised by J.B. Rives (Putnam Classics, 2007).


## CHAPTER 3. THE HERO-KING

"Minos . . . was said by Socrates"—See Plato, *Minos*, Thomas L. Pangle, trans., in Pangle, ed., *The Roots of Political Philosophy* (Cornell, 1987).

"Machiavelli's *The Prince*"—Niccolò Machiavelli, *The Prince*, Harvey C. Mansfield, trans. (University of Chicago Press, 1985; second edition, 1998). Citations are to chapters.

"His sense of 'virtue'"—But note that in describing Agathocles of Syrause (discussed below in Chapter 5), Machiavelli places a limit on what "one can [ ] call virtue" (VIII).

"Timur"—See Beatrice Forbes Mann, *The Rise and Rule of Tamerlane* (Cambridge University Press, 1989). Christopher Marlowe's two-part play *Tamburlaine the Great*, published in 1590, is also of interest. The Shakespeare Theater in Washington, DC, mounted a condensed production in 2007-08.

"Babur"—See *The Baburnama: Memoirs of Babur, Prince and Emperor*, Wheeler M. Thackston, trans. and ed. (Modern Library edition, 2002).

"the end of History"—Alexandre Kojève, *Introduction to the Reading of Hegel*, Allan Bloom, ed. (Basic Books, 1969; Cornell University Press, 1980), 40-41.

"Alexander"—See Plutarch, *Lives*, *Alexander*, Bernadotte Perrin, ed. (G.P. Putnam's Sons, 1916).

"Cyrus"—Xenophon, *The Education of Cyrus*, Wayne Ambler, trans. (Cornell University Press, 2001).

"Gilgamesh"—Stephen Mitchell, *Gilgamesh: A New English Version* (Free Press, 2004). Citations are to the eleven books of Mitchell's division. See also Stephen Dalley, ed., *Myths from Mesopotamia: Creation, The Flood, Gilgamesh, and Others* (Oxford University Press, 1989).

"Rousseau"—Jean-Jacques Rousseau, *Emile: or On Education*, Allan Bloom, trans. (Basic Books, 1979). The quotation is the first sentence of the first chapter of Jean-Jacques Rousseau, *The Social Contract*, Maurice Cranston, trans. (Penguin Books, 1968).

## CHAPTER 4. A HERO'S BARGAIN

"vulnerable when sleeping"—*Leviathan* XIII.

"Joan of Arc"—See Régine Pernoud and Marie-Véronique Clin, *Joan of Arc: Her Story*, Jeremy duQuesnay Adams, trans. (St. Martin's Press, 1998).

"Pompey"—Plutarch, *Lives, Pompey*, Bernadotte Perrin, ed. (G.P. Putnam's Sons, 1916).

"Kojève, drawing on Hegel"—Kojève, *Introduction*, 6, 41.

"Marcellus"—Mary Beard, *The Roman Triumph* (Harvard University Press, 2009), 147-150.

"Crassus"—Plutarch, *Lives, Crassus*, Bernadotte Perrin, ed. (G.P. Putnam's Sons, 1916).

"Round Table"—Wace, *Arthurian Chronicles: Roman de Brut*, Eugene Mason, trans. (Project Gutenberg Ebook, 2003).

"King John"—See Ralph V. Turner, *King John: England's Evil King?* (History Press, 2009).

"*Magna Carta*"—The quotations are from A.E. Dick Howard, *Magna Carta: Text and Commentary* (University of Virginia Press, revised edition, 1998).

"Helsinki Accords became a lever"—See Daniel C. Thomas, *The Helsinki Effect: International Norms, Human Rights, and the Demise of Communism* (Princeton University Press, 2001).

"Wars of the Roses"—See Dan Jones, *The Wars of the Roses: The Fall of the Plantagenets and the Rise of the Tudors* (Viking, second edition, 2014).

"Cromwell"—See Antonia Frasier, *Cromwell* (Grove Press, 2001).

"colonels . . . have figured so prominently"—See Edward N. Luttwak, *Coup d'Etat: A Practical Handbook* (Penguin Press, 1968).

"*Seven Days in May*"—Fletcher Knebel and Charles W. Bailey II, *Seven Days in May* (Harper & Row, 1962).

"McChrystal"—Michael Hastings, "The Runaway General," *Rolling Stone* (June 22, 2010). Helene Cooper and David E. Sanger, "Obama Says Afghan Policy Won't Change After Dismissal," *New York Times* (June 23, 2010).

## CHAPTER 5. HEROISM AND DEMOCRACY

"Perpetual Peace"—See Immanuel Kant, *Perpetual Peace*, in *Political Writings*, H.S. Reiss, ed. (Cambridge University Press, 1970.

"democratic peace"—See Michael W. Doyle, "Liberalism and World Politics," *American Political Science Review* 80:4 (December 1986); John M. Owen, "How Liberalism Produces Democratic Peace," *International Security* 19:2 (Autumn 1994).

"Tocqueville"—Alexis de Tocqueville, *Democracy in America*, Harvey C. Mansfield, trans. (University of Chicago Press, 2000).

"Burke"—The "sanctuary of liberty" quotation is from Burke's "Speech on Moving His Resolutions for Conciliation with the Colonies" (March 22, 1775). He discusses the "natural aristocracy" in "Letter from the New to the Old Whigs" (1791).

"Nietzsche"—The quotations are from Friedrich Nietzsche, *Beyond Good and Evil* in Walter Kaufmann, trans., *Basic Writings of Nietzsche* (Modern Library, Reprint Edition, 1992). The citations are to the book and aphorism number.

"Hegel's dialectic of the master and the slave"—G.W.F. Hegel, *Phenomenology of Spirit*, A.V. Miller, trans. (Oxford University Press, 1977), IV(a).

"How much 'higher' than egalitarian political order . . ."—See Peter Berkowitz, *Nietzsche: The Ethics of an Immoralist* (Harvard University Press, 1995).

## CHAPTER 6. THE BACKLASH AGAINST THE SLAYING HERO

"Jünger"—Ernst Jünger, *On Pain*, David C. Durst, trans. (Telos Press, 2008).

"allegorical novel"—Ernst Jünger, *On the Marble Cliffs*, Stuart Hood, trans. (Penguin, 1984).

"his searing memoir"—Ernst Jünger, *Storm of Steel*, Michael Hofmann, trans. (Penguin, 2004).

"Marshall"—See S.L.A. Marshall, *Men Against Fire: The Problem of Battle Command* (University of Oklahoma Press, 2000).

"a more careful 1987 survey"—Russell W. Glenn, *Reading Athena's Dance Card: Men Against Fire in Vietnam* (Naval Institute Press, 2002).

"The literature of World War I"—The poems quoted here are anthologized in Candace Ward, ed., *World War I British Poets: Brook, Owen, Sassoon, Rosenberg and Others* (Dover, 1997). See also Paul Fussell, *The Great War and Modern Memory* (Oxford University Press, 1975); Robert Graves, *Goodbye to All That: An Autobiography* (Anchor, 1929).

"two lines that create a net loss"—They are: "Obscene as cancer, bitter as the cud / Of vile, incurable sores on innocent tongues—"

"What began as a mostly British"—The section that follows on Vietnam draws from an article of mine, "Of Arms, Men and Monuments," *Commentary* (October 1984), published shortly after the dedication of the Vietnam Veterans Memorial on the Mall in Washington. As will be clear to anyone who thinks it worth the bother to compare the two, some of my views have changed over the 30-year span. Unfortunately, I have been unable to find the citation for the C.D.B. Bryan quotation.

"Mason"—Robert Mason, *Chickenhawk* (Viking, 1983).

"*Charlie Company*"—Peter Goldman and Tony Fuller, *Charlie Company: What Vietnam Did to Us* (William Morrow, 1983).

"MacPherson"—Myra MacPherson, *Long Time Passing: Vietnam and the Haunted Generation* (Doubleday, 1984).

"Terry"—Wallace Terry, *Bloods: An Oral History of the Vietnam War by Black Veterans* (Random House, 1984).

"Mithers"—Carol Mithers, "Picking Up the Pieces," *Village Voice* (May 29, 1984).

"Bowden's 1999 bestseller"—Mark Bowden, *Black Hawk Down: A Story of Modern War* (Atlantic Monthly Press, 1999). The section that follows on the battle of Mogadishu draws from my review-essay on the book, "Men at War," *Policy Review* 95 (June/July 1999).

"Jefferson"—See Fawn M. Brodie, *Thomas Jefferson: An Intimate History* (W.W. Norton, 1974).

"Churchill"—For a recent example, see Michael Dickinson, "Winston Churchill: the Imperial Monster," *Counterpunch* (January 28, 2015).

"Lincoln"—See C.A. Tripp, *The Intimate World of Abraham Lincoln* (Free Press, 2005).

"the radical social determinist position"—See Georgi V. Plekhanov, *The Role of the Individual in History* (1898; University Press of the Pacific, 2003). Marxism was not, of course, the only species of social determinism. See, for example, Karl Lamprecht, *What Is History? Five Lectures on the Modern Science of History* (Macmillan, 1905).

"Hook"—Sidney Hook, *The Hero in History* (1943; Cosimo Classics, 2008).

"If they come to believe that making something of themselves is entirely beyond their power"—See William Damon, *The Path to Purpose: Helping Our Children Find Their Calling in Life* (Free Press, 2008).

"Holden Caulfield"—J.D. Salinger, *Catcher in the Rye* (Little, Brown, 1951).

"OSAMA BIN WANKIN' "—*New York Post* (May 14, 2011).


## CHAPTER 7. VESTIGIAL AND VIRTUAL HEROES

"In the mid-nineteenth century"—This chapter draws from my essay, "From Hero-Worship to Celebrity-Adulation: The Problem of Greatness in an Age of Equality," *Weekly Standard* (October 11, 2011), also published by the Hoover Institution as one in a series of essays on "Endangered Virtues" written by members of the Boyd and Jill Smith Task Force on the Virtues of a Free Society.

"Carlyle"—Thomas Carlyle, *On Heroes, Hero-Worship, and the Heroic in History* (James Fraser, 1841; Echo Library, 2007).

"an expensive sort of low-life behavior"—The source of the anecdote is Kitty Kelley, *His Way: The Unauthorized Biography of Frank Sinatra* (Bantam Press, 1986), 423.

"Tiger Woods"—Maureen Callahan, "The night Tiger Woods was exposed as a serial cheater," *New York Post* (November 24, 2013).

"Quayle"—Andrew Rosenthal, "The 1992 Campaign; Quayle Attacks a 'Cultural Elite,' Saying It Mocks Nation's Values," *New York Times* (June 10, 1992).

"Ibsen"—Henrik Ibsen, *An Enemy of the People* (1882; Amerion, 1967).

"M\*A\*S\*H"—See David S. Reiss, *M\*A\*S\*H: The Exclusive, Inside Story of TV's Most Popular Show* (Macmillan, 1983), and Alan Alda, *Never Have Your Dog Stuffed: And Other Things I've Learned* (Random House, 2005).

"Ion"—Plato, *Ion, Plato in Twelve Volumes* 9, W.R.M. Lamb, trans. (Harvard University Press, 1925).

"Shakespeare, Ibsen, and Shaw"—I took the legendary Ira Kipnis's course on Shaw's plays as an undergraduate at the University of Chicago, and Kipnis attributed this remark to Shaw. I have been unable to find a source, but it's too good to leave out.

"Socrates"—Xenophon, *Apology of Socrates, Xenophon in Seven Volumes* 4, W.R.M. Lamb, trans. (Harvard University Press, 1979). Plato, *Apology, Plato in Twelve Volumes* 1, W.R.M. Lamb, trans. (Harvard University Press, 1966).

"Alcibiades was convicted in absentia"—Thucydides, *History of the Peloponnesian War* VI 61.

"Sodom"—Genesis 19:1-29.

"Putnam"—Robert Putnam, *Bowling Alone* (Simon & Schuster, 2000).

## CHAPTER 8. THE SAVING HERO

"a short story"—See Garrett Stasse, "Ocean Cop Saves Tot," *Atlanticville* (September 29-October 5, 1994) "6-Year-Old Rescued From Blazing Home By Police Officer," *The Coaster* (September 29-October 5, 1994).

"'Sully' Sullenberger"—See Chesley B. Sullenberger, *Highest Duty: My Search for What Really Matters* (William Morrow, 2009)

"The history of the Congressional Medal of Honor"—The Congressional medal of Honor Society maintains a complete list of citations at www.cmohs.org.

"Heidegger"—*Being and Time.*

"amiable or gentle"—Schein, *Mortal Hero*, 35.

"Cicero"—See Anthony Everitt, *Cicero: The Life and Times of Rome's Greatest Politician* (Random House, 2002).

"I have written at some length elsewhere"—Tod Lindberg, *The Political Teachings of Jesus* (HarperOne, 2007).

"Lenny Skutnik"—Sue Anne Pressley Montes, "In a Moment of Horror, Rousing Acts of Courage," *Washington Post* (January 13, 2007).

"two young Marines"—Speech by Marine Lt. Gen. John F. Kelly to the Semper Fi Society of St. Louis on November 13, 2010, excerpted in Scrapbook, *Weekly Standard* (December 6, 2010).

## CHAPTER 9. SACRIFICE AND GENEROSITY

"hardships and dangers"—The passage is in the "Dedicatory Letter" of *The Prince.*

"Porpora"—Douglas V. Porpora, "Personal Heroes, Religion, and Transcendental Metanarratives," *Sociological Forum* 11:2 (1996).

"individual right and reciprocal obligation"—See Alexandre Kojève, *Outline of a Phenomenology of Right*, Bryan-Paul Frost and Robert Howse, trans. (Rowman and Littlefield, 2000).

"negative version of the Golden Rule"—"That which is despicable to you, do not do to your fellow, this is the whole Torah, and the rest is commentary, go and learn it." Rabbi Hillel, in *Babylonian Talmud, Shabbath*, Folio 31a.

"the expression of power . . . has changed"—See Michel Foucault, *Discipline and Punish*, Alan Sheridan, trans. (Vintage Books, second edition, 1995).

## CHAPTER 10. THE RETURN OF THE SLAYING HERO?

"The 'end of History' vogue"—The article that touched off the controversy, and on which the previously cited book was based, was Francis Fukuyama, "The End of History?" *The National Interest* (Summer 1989).

"seers of globalization"—See, for example, Michael Mandelbaum, *The Road to Global Prosperity* (Simon and Schuster, 2014).

"Not least in love with the führer was . . . Heidegger"—See my review of Emmanuel Faye, *Heidegger: The Introduction of Nazism into Philosophy*, Michael B. Smith, trans. (Yale University Press, 2009) in *Commentary* (March 2010).

"'cosmopolitan right'"—Kant, *Perpetual Peace.*

"33 miners . . . in Chile"—See Héctor Tobar, *Deep Down Dark: The Untold Stories of 33 Men Buried in a Chilean Mine, and the Miracle That Set Them Free* (Farrar, Strauss and Giroux, 2014).

"Khmer Rouge"—Samantha Power, *A Problem from Hell: America and the Age of Genocide* (Basic Books, 2002; Perennial, 2003), 87-154.

"LA police officers"—*Report of the Independent Commission on the Los Angeles Police Department* (1991).

"Adis Medunjanin"—Mosi Secret, "Man Convicted of a Terrorist Plot to Bomb Subways Is Sent to Prison for Life," *New York Times* (November 16, 2012).

# INDEX